# Devotions for Job Seekers

# Devotions for Job Seekers

*Daily Encouragement
Along the Way*

Richard Malone

Galilee/Doubleday

NEW YORK  LONDON  TORONTO  SYDNEY  AUCKLAND

A GALILEE BOOK

PUBLISHED BY DOUBLEDAY

a division of Random House, Inc.

GALILEE and DOUBLEDAY are registered trademarks
of Random House, Inc., and the portrayal of a
ship with a cross above a book is a trademark of
Random House, Inc.

*Devotions for Job Seekers* was originally published by
Crossings Book Club as *You're Not Alone* in 1992.

First Galilee edition published October 2003

*Book design by Jennifer Ann Daddio*

Library of Congress Cataloging-in-Publication Data
Malone, Richard.
    [You're Not alone]
    Devotions for job seekers : daily encouragement
along the way / Richard Malone.
        p.    cm.
    Originally published: You're not alone. Nashville, Tenn.:
T. Nelson Publishers, c1992.
    1. Unemployed—Prayer-books and devotions—English.
2. Devotional calendars.   I. Title.
BV4596.U53M25  2003
242'.68—dc21              2003044831

ISBN 0-385-50980-4

# Acknowledgments

Grateful thanks is due to those who read parts of these writings along the way and provided ideas and substantial encouragement, including Ron Beers, Susan Brophy, Susan Heuser, Steve Laube, Michelle Rapkin, and Ann Spangler. Thanks also to the folks at Thomas Nelson who accepted the idea: Lonnie Hull and Ken Stephens when they saw an early manuscript, and the rest before they even knew who the writer was.

A special long-term thank you is due Jim Edwards at Evangel College, who encouraged me to write when I barely knew the difference between a participle and a paragraph.

Finally, my family—Sue, Dan, and David—deserve significant credit for putting up with my sleepy evenings so that I could have alert mornings.

# Introduction

During wartime the greatest fear families face is the knock on the door from someone in a military uniform. That knock normally signals the death of a son or husband. Today employees, likewise, have increasingly come to dread Friday afternoon announcements or conversations with the boss. Too often they signal the death of a job through a merger, consolidation, or downsizing process.

In my case it started out as a simple informal meeting with my supervisor. He got to the point quickly and told me I would lose my job in a reorganization. I was told my position needed someone with a different set of skills. I felt as if I had walked into a room and then couldn't find an exit. It couldn't be. If there was a way in, there surely must be some way out. It didn't make sense. Part of me denied what was happening even as it happened.

I pounded the steering wheel in anger and frustration all the way home. I wondered if I was going to end up in an unemployment line with the Southeastern Michigan auto workers. When I got home I told my family the news, and then sat dazed for the entire evening in front of the TV in a state of stunned shock.

The next morning I tried playing basketball with my normal Saturday morning group of guys. I had to quit after a few minutes, because it was clear I had no energy for even the most modest of athletic competition.

The next few months often found me at some of the

lowest points of my life. What had started out as a simple five-minute conversation turned into a week-long shock treatment. From that point, the experience developed into a long-term, wrenching upheaval of my mind, emotions, and spirit. The implications of what happened seemed to reach every part of my person. It's not hard to see why. I lost part of my identity. I was forced to completely rethink my career and future. My self-confidence was shaken to the core. I was forced to explore options that, frankly, scared me. What I didn't want in the least, I received in full.

I went through three discernible stages similar to a grief crisis. After the first few days of shock, I had to go through the long struggle of adjusting to a new career direction. I also found that the process didn't end when I found new employment. I found a new job rather quickly. But in my new job, the "fresh start" was influenced by residual effects from the shock and struggle. Those effects seemed to be just under or near the surface long after I had established myself in the new job. The crisis feelings lingered longer than I would have expected.

As I went through this tremendous change, I looked for help in a devotional format. I had a difficult time finding applicable material, so I started to write, first motivated almost entirely by my own frustration and then later because others expressed an interest in the same issues: The purpose of this book, then, is to be a devotional resource in that time of crisis. Getting "on track" mentally and emotionally is critical to the process of getting a new job and making a new start. Much of that process takes place when the job seeker is alone, thinking and contemplating the past and future. These devotionals are meant to provide a healthy diet of thoughtful input for those meditative times.

The first part of the book is meant to bring the raw feelings out in the open—to put them on a level of consciousness where we can process them. If we don't do this, then the centrifugal force of all the various emotions will make it increasingly difficult to search for a new job or make the necessary adjustments when we accept a new job.

The middle section is intended to provide a resource for the experiences associated with the struggle of finding a new job. Waiting is often painful and we become terribly impatient. But this also can be a concentrated time of learning.

The final group of devotionals moves into topics that are designed to help the reader consolidate and articulate what he or she learns through the upheaval and adjustments. It will help you make a healthy start in a new job.

When I started to write, I asked, "What does Scripture have to say about job changes?" Surprisingly enough, what I found was that many biblical characters struggled through the same kinds of changes we have, often involuntarily. Sometimes it was because of their own mistakes, sometimes due to circumstances beyond their control, sometimes because God intervened. Such is life, and Scripture gives us that life in a matter-of-fact fashion. Much as Jesus was tempted in all ways as we are, biblical characters also went through the same kinds of job and career changes we have. We can learn from their reactions and from the teaching surrounding the narratives. We can grow in wisdom from the principles in the biblical record.

Each devotional contains a few verses of biblical text. Many times the whole point of the meditation is summed up by that short passage. In some devotionals, however, reading the broader biblical context is helpful to gain the full benefit of seeing God's work in his people's lives. Understanding and identifying with the struggles of those biblical characters is essential to applying the message for us today. Give yourself a chance to identify with these people who struggled as you do by taking some extra time for reading.

Each meditation also contains a brief prayer designed to help you get started in a dialogue with God. You may also find it helpful to write out your own prayers or keep your own journal. Journaling provides openings for God's Holy Spirit to speak to us. Whether we have a lot to say to God or not, getting through a job change goes better as we learn to listen. I encourage you to enter into that dialogue. It will lead to a deeper experience of God's comforting care.

> The secret of overcoming a crisis is the direct result of personal companionship with our Lord, who not only lived triumphantly through his own crisis times but in spirit reveals pathways through our darkest moments as well. (G. Don Gilmore, *No Matter How Dark the Valley*)

# Daily Encouragement for Those Looking for a New Job

# Don't Underestimate
# the Grief

*I am bowed down and brought very low;*
*all day long I go about mourning.*
*My back is filled with searing pain;*
*there is no health in my body.*
                              Psalm 38:6–7 NIV

Even though a job loss throws us into an emotional crisis, we are supposed to pick ourselves up, get out there in the job market quickly, and project enthusiasm, energy, and vitality. The need to be employed as quickly as possible means that we don't have enough time and space to grieve properly. We cannot adequately deal with all the dizzying emotions that spin our minds around.

You probably have already gone through the whole spectrum of emotions. You may still feel that you are in the middle of it now. You may need to retrace some of the thoughts you have had during your job crisis experience. It will be uncomfortable, but it is important to take the time to let God work in you to heal the wounds.

You can expect to mourn. You can expect to go through a grief process that may include several steps. This experience may be one of the roughest you have ever gone through. You have lost a vital part of your life, and nothing short of authentic grieving will allow for a full recovery.

At the same time, don't underestimate God's understanding, care, and provision to help you through the process. You'll find that the Bible was written by people who felt the same kind of grief you do. As you listen to its teaching, you can follow the same process its writers went through to recover from grief.

*Father, please make me whole again. Help me not to shy away from the grief process. Help me to see the necessity of wrestling with all my emotions. Give me the strength to come through this experience a stronger and better person.*

# Feel and Face the Pain

> *In the same way, the Spirit helps us in our weakness.
> We do not know what we ought to pray for, but the
> Spirit himself intercedes for us with groans that words
> cannot express. And he who searches our hearts knows
> the mind of the Spirit, because the Spirit intercedes for
> the saints in accordance with God's will.*
>
> *Romans 8:26–27 NIV*

Ever since my early twenties, I've had periodic bouts with lower back pain. What starts out as minor soreness periodically puts me flat on my back. Any kind of significant movement causes immobilizing pain. So I move as little as possible. When I do have to move, the back pain often makes me come out with groans that take the place of normal vocabulary.

Similarly, the pain connected with losing a job can also immobilize us. Every morning when we get up, it is still there. It too brings on inner groans of anguish. The more we think about it, the more acutely we feel it. We feel like relief should come eventually, but what are we going to do in the meantime? And what if relief doesn't come? We're unsure how we ought to pray, because we don't understand what God is doing.

Take great comfort in Paul's words to the Romans. God evidently expects you to groan a little. He expects that you won't always know how to pray. He gave us the Holy Spirit to meet this need. He understands your mind, your heart, and your emotions even if you can't find the words to express your feelings. The Holy Spirit intercedes for you when you are verbally helpless. It doesn't matter if you don't know how to pray. The Holy Spirit will do it for you.

> These unutterable sighs or groans are not to be despised, as if we ought to put them into language. On the contrary, when we thus sigh with inarticulate desires, it is the Holy Spirit Himself interceding on our behalf prompting these groans. We should not be ashamed of such wordless prayers.
>
> JOHN STOTT, *MEN MADE NEW*

*Father, when these painful times surround me, remind me of what the Holy Spirit does for me. Let me feel the divine comfort that he gives as he intercedes for me. May it give me confidence to face the pain and move through it.*

# Don't Give in
# to Fear   SAYS God 300 t.mes!

> *"Then I said to you, 'Do not be terrified or afraid of
> them. The LORD your God, who goes before you, He
> will fight for you, according to all He did for you in
> Egypt before your eyes, and in the wilderness.'"*
>
> *Deuteronomy 1:29–31 NKJV*

Starting with this passage in Deuteronomy, the Bible
contains the statement ("Do not be afraid") or ("Do not
fear") more than 300 times. Most of these passages occur
when God's people confront something new. In a job
change, much of the fear we have comes from facing new
circumstances. If we're not used to changing jobs, we
may be afraid of possible loss of income, loss of prestige
and reputation, potential loss of assets, loss of future pro-
motions, idle time without a job, or the loss of the security of knowing the source of the next paycheck.

In many of the passages that say, "Do not be afraid,"
the reason given is that God is who he says he is and he
will be with us. Included is a specific promise to us. God
wants us to believe that he is looking out for us.

Unfortunately, I haven't been able to find a thermo-
stat switch anywhere on me that allows me to turn those
feelings down or off. While I want to believe, the fears
linger. FACE the Fear Identify it & Command out

But these passages of Scripture give us concrete steps
Away
to take as we find fear a part of our daily emotions. I
& gone!

6

don't need to change the feelings as if I had a switch on them. What I can do is seek to know God better through Scripture and prayer. That growing knowledge makes it possible for the Holy Spirit to counsel me to trust God and his promises.

Trusting God means that we believe that God is at work through the occasion of our pain for our ultimate good.

JERRY BRIDGES, *TRUSTING GOD*

Lord, when fear starts to dominate my thinking, work through your Holy Spirit to remind me of all your promises. I confess that too many of them are far-off abstractions. I need to believe them personally. Be God, the Holy Spirit, in my life. Take away my fears and comfort me with your presence.

7

# Grace Is the Antidote
to Loneliness

*I am lonely and troubled.*
*Show that you care*
*    and have pity on me.*
*My awful worries keep growing.*
*Rescue me from sadness.*
*See my troubles and misery*
*    and forgive my sins.*
            Psalm 25:16–18 CEV

A friend told me that one of the hardest aspects of her layoff was the loss of relationships. She felt an awkwardness in being with her old workmates outside the normal work context because the social setting was so different. She still valued the relationships, yet found them difficult to maintain once her employment ended. The result was a loneliness that hit her the hardest at 8:30 on Monday mornings.

Loneliness can attack us like an enemy. It can drain us emotionally and physically like a virulent strain of Asian flu. Like a long bout with the flu, it can also steal the emotional resources we need to find a new job.

The psalmist points us to God's grace as the solution to loneliness. We tend to see grace too much as a theological term that applies only to a salvation experience. While the theme of "Amazing Grace" is central to its understanding, a more accurate biblical picture of grace is bigger. Grace encompasses every aspect of our lives, not just the spiritual. We receive God's grace as whole people throughout our whole lives, not just as a single isolated experience at the time we actually become Christians.

Grace can also function as an antidote to loneliness. The depth of God's grace meets the depths of our loneliness. Grace implies protection. Grace leads to freedom from stress. Grace is God's supporting and healing activity in our lives in the midst of difficulty and disaster.

*Lord, help me to see all the facets of grace that are available to me. My own shortsightedness limits my seeing that your grace can heal in my life. When I miss my job, when I miss the people I worked with, may your grace provide a healing balm for my wounded heart.*

# Failure Does Not Need to Be the End of the Story

> *Immediately the rooster crowed the second time. Then Peter remembered the word Jesus had spoken to him: "Before the rooster crows twice you will disown me three times." And he broke down and wept.*
>
> Mark 14:72 NIV

> *And he said to Him, "Lord, You know all things; You know that I love You."*
>
> John 21:17 NKJV

Scripture has some marvelous stories of success. Joseph and Daniel seem to defy the difficulties of their circumstances to rise to the top socially and politically. From a start in slavery, they both achieved greatness in powerful positions of influence.

Scripture also contains dramatic stories of failures: David chasing after Bathsheba; Moses losing his chance to enter the Promised Land; Peter denying Christ. At the root of each of these failures is disobedience or a failure to trust God. At the center of the successes is trust.

In denying Christ, Peter failed about as dramatically as anyone could. After three years of following Christ, he forgot the most basic lesson: Trust the Master. Fortunately, God is used to dealing with failures. In the last chapter of John's Gospel, we see a forgiven Peter, reinstated and eager to prove his loyalty to Jesus.

Sooner or later most of us will fail at something: a job, our own business, a major project. Sometimes the problem may have been bad judgment or circumstances beyond our control. Sometimes it may be that we honestly blew it. God isn't surprised. Our failures may separate us from a job, but not from his love.

*Father, if I'm at fault, help me to accept the blame. Help me to be honest about and responsible for my failures. Help me understand the mistakes I made. Then give me motivation and courage to change what I can and accept what I cannot.*

# Dealing with Bitterness

*We are sure about all this. Christ makes us sure in the very presence of God. We don't have the right to claim that we have done anything on our own. God gives us what it takes to do all that we do. He makes us worthy to be the servants of his new agreement that comes from the Holy Spirit and not from a written Law. After all, the Law brings death, but the Spirit brings life.*

*2 Corinthians 3:4–6 CEV*

Bitterness over: being used up, not being warned, not being appreciated for our accomplishments, being shoved aside, being forced to change abruptly, being judged unfairly, being taken for granted, not being understood.

It happens to all of us. At some point, no matter how hard we have worked, we realize that our accomplishments just don't seem to mean much. We wonder what we could have done differently. We go through a lot of "what if" scenarios in our minds. Our self-esteem is deflated like a week-old party balloon. When we ask ourselves why, the answers seldom satisfy.

One of the interesting recurring events in Paul's ministry was his constant need to defend himself. We see the evidence of this in several of his letters to the churches. Some of these churches made life miserable for him, even though he had spent months pouring himself out for them. How did he keep from feeling bitter in these circumstances? Second Corinthians 3:4–6 offers a perspective that provides a basis for Paul to deal with these kinds of situations. He is fully aware that his accomplishments are a result of the grace of God. The net result is that his confidence is less in himself and more in God. He had what could be called a God-centered self-esteem. Events and circumstances didn't shape his attitude as much as his relationship with God did. As a result, he had a healthy way to deal with the negative feedback or situations that often cause bitterness. He could state his cause, knowing that God understood and that God was in charge.

*God, make me more aware of how your plans and my work fit together: Help me understand the traits you're developing in me. Give me a God-centered confidence that is not disturbed by criticism and negative feedback.*

# God as a Punching Bag

*Surely I have cleansed my heart in vain,*
*And washed my hands in innocence.*
                    Psalm 73:13 NKJV

Where do you go with anger when you lose a job? If you're still working for the same company, expressing that anger probably won't do much more than reconfirm the thoughts of those responsible for the change. If you express anger as you leave the company, you may foolishly burn a bridge to any future possibilities. Expressing anger to those who have no direct knowledge may get you some sympathy, but that doesn't go far. The problem with expressing anger is that we can never be sure that we have been understood. We also can hurt ourselves or other people in a way that we will regret. Like a frustrated young adolescent, we need a punching bag that gives us a way to express anger without hurting someone.

God provides himself. If there was ever anything we should bring to God, it's anger. He hears us. He won't misinterpret us. He won't think any less of us for expressing anger. He knows what's behind it. He knows the causes better than we do. He knows if our anger is justified. He has experienced the same kind of rejection that makes us feel angry.

We find the psalmists expressing all kinds of anger, some of it outright violent. Psalm 73 contains a confession of a time when that anger got the best of the psalmist, and he expressed it to God. There is nothing in the record to indicate that God rejects this anger. In fact anger seems to be accepted as one of the steps that the writer goes through in order to get to the place where he can confirm God's goodness and sovereignty. God's grace is big enough to accept our anger.

> Anger should not be destroyed but sanctified.
> WILLIAM JENKYN,<br>*THE GOLDEN TREASURY*<br>*OF PLYMOUTH QUOTATIONS*

*Help me, Jesus, to bring my anger to you. There's not one part of it that you don't understand. You know all the causes and all the effects. I can trust you not to hold what I say or feel against me in the future. And best of all, I know that you're there to hear me at any time and in any circumstance.*

# Revenge Is Not So
# Sweet After All

*Dear friends, don't try to get even. Let God take revenge. In the Scriptures the Lord says,*

*"I am the one to take revenge and pay them back."*

*Romans 12:19 CEV*

You may remember when Lee Iacocca brought Chrysler back from near bankruptcy in the early 1980s. He often stated that one of his primary motives for success at Chrysler was to get revenge at Henry Ford II for firing him. While one can make a case that he succeeded, it was a short-lived kind of revenge. Chrysler did become profitable under Iacocca. The minivan idea that Ford rejected became a trend-setting success at Chrysler. But Henry Ford II died in 1987. Now, years later, Chrysler is still the number three U.S. auto maker. In the total scheme of life, revenge as a motivation has profound limits. Even if we meet our goals, the smug satisfaction that comes with it is at best a fleeting emotion.

Paul understood this and makes it clear in his letter to the Romans that revenge is not compatible with Christian character. It seems almost inevitable that during a career, we will be taken for granted at some point. We will be mistreated sometimes. Our contributions will not be recognized fully. Scripture teaches us that we may not go to another job with an attitude of revenge as a motive. If we were treated unjustly, God promises to carry out judgment for us.

*Remind me, Lord, that I have no business playing God and taking revenge. You're in charge of distributing justice, not me. When I start to think of getting back at someone, help me to replace those thoughts with ideas that are constructive rather than destructive. In all work situations, may my motives be to serve you.*

# In Times of Depression, Use God's Safety Net

> *But he said to me, "My grace is sufficient for you, for my power is made perfect in weakness." Therefore I will boast all the more gladly about my weaknesses, so that Christ's power may rest on me.*
>
> *2 Corinthians 12:9 NIV*

Last year, a manager I knew took his own life in a motel. He had become especially despondent over the last two years. He had been turned down for an advancement in his company. He had become more and more depressed. He felt he had nowhere to go and that his family was better off without him. He had standards and goals for himself that he couldn't attain, and he couldn't let God's grace cover his disappointment. He must have felt that he had lost the fight.

He was the kind of person who always faced the dollar bills the same direction in his wallet. His wastebasket was probably neater than my desk. It is hard to imagine anyone more organized. But there was no place for failure in his personal organization, and there needed to be. He needed to know that God makes provision for our failure.

God's grace provides a safety net for the farthest of falls. Most of us should expect to use that net at some point in our lives.

The screams of depression should never be allowed to drown out the whisperings of God's assurance of His love for us and His presence with us.

DON BAKER, *DEPRESSION,*
*FINDING HOPE AND MEANING IN*
*LIFE'S DARKEST SHADOW*

*Father, sometimes I feel like I'm falling into a dangerous pit of depression. I can't pull myself up by my bootstraps. My hands can't keep a grip and my strength is completely depleted. I'm desperate for help. I don't have answers to my problems. Give me the grace to accept myself, all my failures, my weaknesses, and inadequacies. Help me to see the safety net today and that you assure its security.*

# You Are Not as Helpless
## as You Think

*God is our refuge and strength,*
*A very present help in trouble.*
                    Psalm 46:1 NKJV

When news reporters read the monthly unemployment statistics, they often add a comment about the fact that many of the unemployed have also given up the search. The implication is that reality is probably worse than the statistics. Every month, more people join the ranks of those who feel helpless in finding a job.

What do you do when you are utterly helpless to change the circumstances that have caused a job loss? How do you overcome the thoughts of "what's the use?" The psalmists would say, "Rely on the one whose very nature is one of helpfulness." Psalm 46 lays out the qualities of his help. It's strong enough to meet the need. It is always there, no matter how great the disaster. It's there when we need it, when we're in trouble.

These words were written when the entire nation of Israel was in danger of becoming extinct. Israel faced constant threats from nations that sought to overrun her, such as Egypt and Assyria. The Israelites knew all about being helpless. Some of their most desperate situations became their most dramatic rescues. God's strategy for helping the Israelites included fire, clouds, the Red Sea, quail, manna from heaven, water from a rock, and a wall-toppling earthquake. God can help, using anything at any time. We are not, nor will we ever be, helpless.

*These words of Psalm 46, Lord, are like finding an available taxi on a late night in a dangerous part of town. Help me to understand that no matter how great the disaster I experience, you can provide the help to overcome it. Encourage me with your helpfulness.*

# Can It Get Any Worse?

> *Then David said to all his officials who were with him in Jerusalem, "Come! We must flee, or none of us will escape from Absalom. We must leave immediately, or he will move quickly to overtake us and bring ruin upon us and put the city to the sword."*
>
> 2 Samuel 15:14 NIV, read 2 Samuel 15

If you ask anyone to recount the worst day of his life, often he will tell you about the day he lost his job. If you asked David to remember the worst day of his life, he likely would have recounted the day he lost his job as king and had to move out of his palace in Jerusalem. At that point David had ruled Israel for more than twenty years. He had brought stability to Israel in a way it had never seen before. The people should have been profoundly grateful to the man who had endured countless battles and Saul's persecution on his way to becoming king. Instead, they told him to clean out his desk.

David's son, Absalom, proved to be a better politician than his father and won over the hearts of much of the nation. The result was a coup that had David running for his life. Didn't David deserve better? Certainly he did, but that doesn't seem to be how life works, even for God's most valued servants. Serious setbacks occur. Why? The most simple answer seems to be that God's plans are different from ours. Should we be surprised? Probably not, but we often are. We are told by the world to take control of our lives, and we forget who's really in control.

Learning how little control we have, in such a startling way, can be depressing. It can also be comforting because we quickly realize that even though God's plans may differ from ours, He will get us where he wants us, no matter what it takes. I might as well make up my mind to enjoy the journey. I may not know the details of the itinerary, but I know who planned the trip, and he doesn't make mistakes.

*Right now, Lord, I feel like I have few reasons to look positively on the future. Major parts of my life seem completely out of sync. Remind me that the future is yours in every sense of the word. Help me find where I fit in your plans.*

# It's Not Fair

*Then Joseph's master took him and put him into the*
*prison, a place where the king's prisoners were confined.*
*Genesis 39:20 NKJV*

A friend who recently lost his job commented that he used to think if he worked hard and met his goals, employers would always be happy with him and he would be successful. He found out that hard work is often overshadowed by capricious decisions among owners or managers.

Is it right? No. Is it fair? No. Does it even make sense? Perhaps not. But it happens to a lot of us. It happened to Joseph too. He had made the most of being sold as a slave by working hard and meeting all of his owner's expectations. He proved himself to be a superb employee only to be bumped entirely off the ladder of success.

The writer of Genesis left out any record of how Joseph felt. Joseph had already made a new life for himself once. His emotions must have been a mixture of anger, bewilderment, and utter frustration. How could God expect him to start over again?

For most of us, the power of those emotions keeps us from seeing or believing that God is still in control of our discouraging circumstances. Maybe we won't understand the reasons for a while. It could take years, as it did in Joseph's case, for God's plan to become understandable, but we can trust him to take care of the big picture.

*Lord, in the midst of swirling emotions, help me to be faithful to you. Remind me of Joseph's example. Help me to be true to it, trusting you and looking to the future you control and the answers you will provide.*

# A Sense of Loss

*Because of the LORD's great love we are not consumed,*
*for his compassions never fail.*

Lamentations 3:22 NIV

One of the most dominant feelings we have when we change jobs is a sense of loss. We lose a sense of accomplishment. We lose the equity we have built up in relationships with people. We lose the professional niche that we have carved out for ourselves.

Some of those same kinds of feelings are expressed poignantly in the book of Lamentations. In five short chapters (which make a great week's worth of reading), the author portrays individuals and a whole nation who have experienced the loss of their land and with it much of their identity. The sense of grief is almost overwhelming. "Almost," because within these verses there is also a powerful expression of God's supportive care.

The fourth chapter, particularly, contains a compelling affirmation of God's sustaining love. While God allowed the captivity of Israel to take place, he didn't completely abandon his people. The Israelites lost much of what was near and dear to them, but they didn't lose God. Verse 22 states it well: "We are not consumed." We may be frustrated. We may be deeply hurt. We may not have any idea how we're going to handle the problems we face, but we are not consumed. We are not shriveling up to nothing. God's sustaining love saw the Israelites through the Exile until they were able to return to their land. He will see us through our most difficult periods until we find a new niche.

There is no pit so deep that He is not deeper still.

CORRIE TEN BOOM,
*THE HIDING PLACE*

*Lord, when thoughts of what I've lost overwhelm me, remind me of all that I still have in you. Remind me that what you provide are the important things. See me through when I can't see my own way through.*

# Feelings of Worthlessness

*Praise the God and Father of our Lord Jesus Christ for the spiritual blessings that Christ has brought us from heaven!*

*Ephesians 1:3* CEV

"You're worth it," proclaims the hair treatment commercial. But a job crisis often makes you wonder what you *are* worth. Losing a job may affect your self-confidence for the rest of your life.

You do need to know what you're worth to employers. You want to know and be able to articulate the ways you perform well at work. You gain a certain amount of pleasure from the tasks you do well. But you also need to know what you are worth to God and respond to that. He is the source of our ultimate satisfaction.

We can tell our worth in God's sight by what he has done and still promises to do on our behalf. As we read Ephesians 1, we feel like it's Christmas, we have been to Grandma's house, and she's given us so much we can't even get it all in the car to go home. We are worth so much to God that he has heaped treasures on us. He has blessed and chosen us. He has adopted us to be his children. He redeems and forgives us. He has made a perfect plan for us. He has given us the Holy Spirit, who is a deposit guaranteeing our inheritance. He has given us every spiritual blessing we can imagine and more.

Our worth to God has nothing to do with what we do to make a living. It has only to do with his generosity, and in that we participate 100 percent, no matter what our job is.

*Lord, don't let me forget how much I'm worth to you. Remind me constantly of what you did to demonstrate your love for me. May that understanding root out the feelings of inadequacy that I have.*

# Distressed and Restless

*When I was in distress, I sought the Lord;*
*At night I stretched out untiring hands*
*and my soul refused to be comforted.*
                                                      *Psalm 77:2 NIV*

The grief of losing a job puts our souls in a state of distress. There is often little anyone can say to comfort us. Sympathy from friends and relatives helps some, but it doesn't provide lasting solace. Like the psalmist, we stretch out our hands to God for comfort, but have difficulty receiving the help he gives. Spiritually, we're like the baby who can't get to sleep when she's too tired. Somehow our neediness is a barrier to seeing all the resources that are available to us. We want comfort. We need it, yet it eludes us.

We raise the same kinds of questions the psalmist does. Where is God's compassion? Has he forgotten me? Have I done something to cause God to reject me?

The psalmist's answer is to catalog the mighty acts of God, his miracles, his power over nature. By taking this action, we too remember that God does act, that he powerfully demonstrates his care for those who trust him. He leads his people through the most difficult of circumstances and the most trying of times. He will do no less for us.

The people of Israel were up against impossible odds when they found themselves between the chariots of Egypt and the Red Sea. Their God is our God. The God of Israel and our God looks down on us with love and says, "Nothing has happened to you which is not common to all. I can mandate it. Trust me."

ELISABETH ELLIOT,
*A PATH
THROUGH SUFFERING*

*Lord, help me to make the transition from restlessness to restfulness in you. Change my feelings of distress to expectation for the fulfillment of your promises. Part my Red Sea and lead me on the dry path. Bring me water in my desert and cause me to drink deeply.*

# Facing Rejection

> *But as soon as Jeremiah finished telling all the people*
> *everything the LORD had commanded him to say, the*
> *priests, the prophets and all the people seized him and*
> *said, "You must die!"*
>
> *Jeremiah 26:8 NIV*

Rejection was an occupational hazard for the prophets. Jeremiah's experience was no exception. When he went to the people of Judah with God's message, they wanted to kill him. They weren't satisfied with telling him to get lost. They wanted to throw him off the city wall.

Jeremiah faced rejection with a bold confidence because of the clear direction he had from God. Most of us don't have as definite a call. We don't have the word of the Lord burning on our tongues the way Jeremiah did. So how do we cope?

We cope in a crisis by making the knowledge of God's love fit into our thought patterns. When you feel utterly rejected, remember the cross and the rejection Jesus experienced for our eternal security. When you feel nobody cares what happens to you, remember that God knows how many hairs you have and what has happened to all the ones you've lost.

Jeremiah knew in part what Paul lived and taught in depth. Nothing can separate us from God's love. Human rejection can be devastating. But it can never have the last word. God has the last word, and that word is grace.

For I am persuaded that neither death nor life, nor angels nor principalities not powers, nor things present nor things to come, nor height nor depth, nor any other created thing, shall be able to separate us from the love of God which is in Christ Jesus our Lord.

ROMANS 8:38–39 NKJV

*Loving Father, when I feel rejection pulling me down, remind me of your acceptance. Even though you had ample reason to reject me, you didn't. I praise you for being a God of grace. May the balm of your grace heal my feelings of rejection.*

# When Disillusionment
# Gets to You

> *But I almost stumbled and fell,*
> *    because it made me jealous*
> *to see proud and evil people*
> *    and to watch them prosper.*
> *They never have to suffer; they stay healthy, . . .*
> *It was hard for me to understand all this!*
> *Then I went to your temple,*
> *    and there I understood*
> *what will happen to my enemies.*
>                     Psalm 73:2–3, 16–17 CEV

You took the job, thinking things were going to be different at this company. You hoped the management here practiced justice with its employees. After a few months, you found that political conditions weren't much different than your previous place of employment.

You continue to be amazed at what the sneaky often get away with. It seems that they get unjustified credit because they have a talent for creating the perception of good performance. At the same time, they have an uncanny ability to put distance between themselves and failure. They can work a kind of subtle, deceitful shell game to perfection. They know how to win the favor of the boss, when you're happy if he remembers your name.

We feel let down when people who get ahead are those whose work is characterized by flash and dash rather than substance. It seems that an ounce of political skill can get a person farther than a pound of plain, old-fashioned hard work.

This phenomenon gets to the psalmist too. He says he almost loses his bearings when he observes the easy life of the wicked. He doesn't understand how they can ignore God and continue to increase their wealth. He is disillusioned until he enters God's sanctuary to worship.

How does worship remove feelings of disillusion-ment?

Worship puts us in contact with what will last: our God. In worship, reality and substance come to the front, while deception recedes. Its shallowness and in-compatibility with truth become more obvious. Worship exposes the heart and brings it to a place where God can heal it.

*Thank you, Lord, that you always make a way for me to come and worship you. Thank you that your Holy Spirit continually draws me to yourself. Replace the disillusionment I feel with the confidence that comes from your nearness. Replace my weakness with your strength in me.*

# Feeling Alone and Abandoned

*I cry out day and night,*
*but you don't answer, and I can never rest.*
                                *Psalm 22:2 CEV*

A female friend told me that when she lost her job, she felt an overwhelming sense of abandonment. Subtly, she said, she had let the job take on the role of a provider in much the same way that a husband would have. She not only depended on the job financially; she also depended on it for self-esteem. It had helped to shape her identity and purpose. When she was laid off, she felt someone had abandoned her and left her to fend for herself. The future departed on the last train, and she wasn't on it.

David expresses similar feelings of abandonment in Psalm 22. To him it feels that God is far away and unable to answer his prayers. He is surrounded by trouble, and his strength is drained. His enemies threaten him and he has nowhere to turn for help. His repeated prayer is "Do not be far from me, for trouble is near and there is no one to help."

But David doesn't stop at expressing his overwhelming feelings. They don't represent the whole picture. David reminds himself of the history of his people and God's provision for them. God's nurturing care reminds him of a nursing mother. Even though David feels a sense of abandonment, his prayer seems to pull the truth of God's steadfast love and care back into his thinking.

God is not surprised at our feelings of abandonment. David felt them. Jesus felt them on the cross. As we try to draw closer to him, he readily answers and comes closer to us. Then we find that he was there for us all the time.

*Don't stay far away, LORD!*
*My strength comes from you, so hurry and help.*
                    PSALM 22:19 CEV

# Fired and Fallen

*To him who is able to keep you from falling and to
present you before his glorious presence without fault
and with great joy . . .*

Jude 24 NIV

The personnel forms say *terminated*. The word on the
shop floor or in the office is *fired*. Either way, the result
is a stigma of fallenness. We're branded with an "F" for
*fired* like Hester Prynne of Hawthorne's *Scarlet Letter*
was branded with an "A" for *adulteress*. We dread every
future interview where our mistakes may be found out.
We feel as if we've fallen into a dark pit with few ways to
climb out and more ways to fall deeper in.

The book of Jude contains a verse that addresses
those feelings. The verse is a doxology, an ascription of
praise to God. It contains a powerful affirmation that
God is able to keep us from falling. When we go through
a job change, he is able to keep us from falling any further into the depths of despair. He is able to keep us
from falling into self-destructive patterns of behavior. He
will keep us from focusing on only the past and present.

He keeps us from falling by preparing us for the future. He reminds us that after sorrow, joy will come. All
the frustrations, guilt, failures, and inadequacies we feel
will be forgotten. Our future with him insists we look
forward not back. Just knowing that our God is this kind
of God gives us hope. He will move us beyond present
circumstances and continue to work in our lives.

*Father, thank you for being more than a God of glory and might. Thank you for the way you anticipate my needs and feelings. Help me to let you be God fully in my life. Help me to look ahead with eager anticipation to all that you have prepared for me in this world and in the world to come.*

# It's Okay to Cry

*Day and night my tears are my only food,*
*as everyone keeps asking,*
*  "Where is your God?"*

*Psalm 42:3 CEV*

His remark surprised me. I repeated it to another friend, and he agreed. In the experience of both men, they cried more when they lost their jobs than when their fathers died.

Some people may think this a sad commentary on father and son relationships. How can anyone let a job become more important than family?

Another response, though, would be to acknowledge the depth of the hurt that comes from losing a job. Jobs often do take over a greater part of our identities than our family heritage, especially in those families where there isn't much heritage to be proud of. In addition, the loss of a parent doesn't usually have the profound effects on the adult child's future that a job loss does.

When we lose a job, we may cry long and hard, more tears than we have shed in years, tears that come on us unexpectedly, tears that come from feeling that a part of our lives is being wrenched from us, tears that blur our vision of God and the future.

Psalm 42 acknowledges the depth of these feelings. The psalmist goes so far as to say that the times of crying have taken the place of his times of eating. He almost feels like God is trying to quench his thirst with human tears.

Between sobs, God raises a question in the psalmist's mind: "Why are you downcast, O my soul? Why so disturbed within me?" Even the slightest movement to answer that question puts him in touch with a caring God. From that touch, hope clears up the tears and points us to a God who does hear, act, and save us. In a job transition, the most powerful action we can take is to nurture our hope in God.

*Father, lately my life seems awash with tears, and I don't know what to do with the feelings that produce those tears. I don't know when I have ever felt such overwhelming sadness. Point me toward the hope that can dry up the tears. Remind me of all the specific instances of care you have already provided. Help me to keep in mind that your reliability is not affected by my tears.*

# God Is for
# the Oppressed

*The LORD also will be a refuge for the oppressed,*
*A refuge in times of trouble.*
*And those who know Your name will put their trust in*
*You;*
*For You, LORD, have not forsaken those who seek You.*
Psalm 9:9–10 NKJV, read Psalm 9

Didn't they understand the key role I played in the success of the department? Did they really think that eliminating my skills wouldn't have much effect on how things ran and on the bottom line? Didn't loyalty and hours of unpaid overtime count for anything? Questions like these eat away at you after losing your job.

You probably will never get satisfactory answers from the people who made the decision. They had their reasons. Some reasons may have been justified, some not. Some may have been made for sound economic reasons that seemed necessary. Some may have been made because of petty personality differences or politics. Some may have been because you got caught in an inevitable reorganization that left you without an advocate. You're out. Someone else is in, and whoever has the power to change the decision is somewhere in an inaccessible black hole.

You end up feeling a deep oppression that not only takes away your job and your income, but also your dignity and self-respect. You wonder, "Is there any way to get justice?"

The psalmist's answer is to seek God. He stands up for the oppressed. He answers those who seek him. There is not one detail about your circumstances that he doesn't understand. He has an open-door policy, and you don't need to give a lengthy explanation. He satisfies temporal questions with the ultimate answer: himself.

*Lord, put a desire in me to seek you. I know you want me to come to you as a refuge. I need that place of safety now. Thank you for being available. Thank you for not only providing answers, but also for being an answer.*

# Identifying with Christ
# Instead of Your Job

*For to me, to live is Christ, and to die is gain.*
*Philippians 1:21 NKJV*

Professional career counselors point out that grief from a job loss is often more devastating than that of a death in the family. Perhaps people are too invested in their jobs. But another reason is that death brings a sense of finality and closure, while a job loss feels open-ended.

When someone in your family dies, you know what you have lost. When you're out of work, you face continual questions about the future. Will you have to move? Will you be able to find work in the same field? Will you be able to go on the vacation you had planned? Will you have to use up all your savings? In a sense, you don't even know exactly what you have lost because you don't know yet how long it will take to find a new job.

Paul's identification with Christ transcended his job and death itself. It would probably be fair to say that he was consumed by his identification with Jesus. He still had an occupation, making tents, but his job wasn't the center of his life. Christ was.

You say, "That's great, now you expect me to think like an apostle too. It took years for Paul to get to that place. How can I expect to get there right now?"

You're right. That kind of identification doesn't normally happen overnight. What's important is knowing that's where God wants you to be and praying for it to take place. I don't think God expects you to get up and put aside all concerns about where the next paycheck is going to come from. He does expect you to pay more attention to his whispers and identify more closely with him. Greater commitment will inevitably lead to greater identification with him.

*Father, I find Paul's example of identifying with Christ rather daunting. Part of me says, "Don't even try to move in that direction because you can't come close." Encourage me. Help me to deal with my feelings of lost identity by learning to identify with Christ.*

# When You Get the Bad News, Turn to God in Worship

> *Naked I came from my mother's womb,*
> *And naked shall I return there.*
> *The LORD gave, and the LORD has taken away;*
> *Blessed be the name of the LORD.*
>
> *Job 1:21–22 NKJV*

When I lost my job, I certainly didn't follow Job's example of worship in the first two days. But by Monday, I could at least say, "I guess I'll have to trust you, Lord." I wasn't used to living with the idea that a job is the Lord's to take away. In my case, I had built my job from the day the company incorporated. I lost sight of the fact that the job was God's gift from the beginning.

It's hard to imagine anyone going through a greater series of shocks than Job did. In a few short minutes he lost his family, his possessions, his way of life. His response is almost shocking. Job's ability to fall down and worship in the midst of personal disaster seems unreal and impractical, but only if we see our jobs as our own. If we see them as Job sees all of his family and possessions—as gifts from God—then worship makes sense as a way of drawing close to that source again from which our jobs and our whole lives come.

The Westminster Catechism says that the chief end of man is to glorify God and enjoy him forever. Gordon Fee, from Regent College, once made the point that in our day we have distorted that statement to read "the chief end of God is to make me feel good and meet my needs forever." The act of worship puts us into that right relationship with God. When we worship we put ourselves into a position where we can see how a job fits into our lives.

> As we express and strengthen our faith through
> praise, we enthrone God in our situation. We tune
> ourselves in to enjoy His sovereign sufficiency.
> God in turn manifests His presence on our behalf
> in both inner and outer ways. He uses our trials as
> a stage on which He displays His love and power
> and faithfulness.

WARREN AND RUTH MYERS, *PRAISE*

*Father, I worship you as a loving and caring God. Help me to see your loving care in the midst of crisis. It's hard to see that anything good can come out of these circumstances. Help me to keep my conviction that you are Lord and deserve my praise.*

# Understand God's Bigness

> *Where were you when I laid the earth's foundation?*
> *Tell me, if you understand.*
> *Who marked off its dimensions? Surely you know!*
> *Who stretched a measuring line across it?*
>
> Job 38:4–5 NIV

It's easy to let our personal world become the whole world when we experience a disaster. Subtly (or sometimes blatantly) we project our helpless feelings onto God. We wonder why he couldn't or didn't act on our behalf.

It's not easy to be brought up short by an angry God when we feel we have good reason to be angry at him. Yet this is precisely what happens to Job. After Job and his friends discuss all the possible reasons for Job's disaster for more than thirty chapters, the ultimate conclusion is that God is bigger than our disasters. The question of "why" is answered only by the "who."

In chapter 42 Job seems so subdued—it's as if he's been crushed down to a heap of repentant ashes. We say, "Isn't that a little extreme? Does his dignity have to be taken along with everything else? Isn't there a more gentle way? After all, he is already hurting. What do you expect, God? He's only human."

"That's the point," God says. Our starting point has to be that we are human and God is God. We need to understand how presumptuous we are, how much we expect God to be at our beck and call. Without that basic understanding, we have no foundation on which to re-build.

> Those who know God come to recognize that it is better to know God and to trust God than to claim the rights of God.
>
> D. A. CARSON, *HOW LONG, O LORD?*

*Father, forgive me for my presumptuousness. Help me to understand that I'm the creature and you're the Creator. I repent of any attitude that would be less than that. I know there will be moments when this attitude will seem absurd to me and I'll rebel against it. Help me accept the posture of bended knee because that's the position that makes your view of the world visible.*

# Trust God's Plan

*I know that you can do all things;*
*no plan of yours can be thwarted.*
                    Job 42:2 NIV

Planning has almost become a cult in our culture. In many companies, employees carry around notebook-sized organizers in order to keep all their schedules and "To Do" lists straight. Palm Pilots and other PDA's (or Personal Digital Assistants) have become favorite tools of technologically oriented business people. Planning software is regularly used for projects of many kinds. It is common to see large wall charts and calendars that lay out plans for months at a time. Seminars are available constantly on the subjects of different kinds of planning. Consultants specialize in long-term and long-range strategic planning.

While I doubt Job had a day-timer, he probably did have significant plans for his future. Personal disaster wasn't on the agenda. It never is, but it happens so frequently, you'd think we would acknowledge its possibility more readily. We can plan our lives to the last detail, and still we have to agree with Job that God can do whatever he wants. Our plans may be entirely thwarted, but his will not. We don't like hearing that because *we* want to be in charge. The book of Job reminds us that we're not.

*God, I don't think I like what you have put on my agenda for now. I'm uneasy about my future. I feel like I've lost control of my life. Teach me to trust you. Help me to know that the plans you have for me are far better than anything I could imagine. May my number one agenda be to love you with my whole mind, heart, and strength.*

# Struggling to Grow

*It is never fun to be corrected. In fact, at the time it is always painful. But if we learn to obey by being corrected, we will do right and live at peace.*

*Hebrews 12:11 CEV*

While the primary struggle that takes place during a job crisis is to find new work to get the income flowing again, most of us struggle on several other levels. One level is our dependence on and trust in God. We struggle to apply our faith very practically to our everyday lives in areas where we have always been independent and self-reliant. We also struggle with why we lost our job. Often we remember events and decisions we could have controlled or changed but didn't. Still another is the struggle to reestablish an identity that exists completely apart from our work.

For many this time is one of the deepest crisis points in our lives. While it can be tremendously difficult, it can also be a time of unmatched spiritual growth in our lives. God has us where he wants us: dependent on him, listening to him. During this crisis we can learn new patterns of relating to him that will improve the whole remainder of our lives. We can prepare to insert some new attitudes into our work which will make us better employees. While the struggle isn't always pleasant, it is always rewarding if we grow in our relationship with God.

Scripture gives us numerous examples of people who struggled and strong teaching on the principles of dealing with the struggle. The Word equips us for the contest. We may feel as if we're in a lifeboat, far from land. But we find that the boat is well equipped with provisions and direction-finding gear to carry us into our home port.

*Lord Jesus, while I want to grow, I'm not at all fond of the process I have to go through to grow. Help me to see your Word as the equipment I need to sustain that growth. Help me apply it to my life in a way that will make me a better worker for you and any future employer I might have.*

# Depending on God

*Moses also said, "You will know that it was the LORD*
*when he gives you meat to eat in the evening and all*
*the bread you want in the morning, because he has*
*heard your grumbling against him. Who are we? You*
*are not grumbling against us, but against the LORD."*
*Exodus 16:8 NIV, read Exodus 16*

One of the most difficult and yet indispensable lessons
we have to learn, when our career paths lead us into a period of unemployment, is how to be dependent on God.
We would like to be in control of our own destiny. We'd
like the security of an increasing salary level for at least
the next ten years. We'd like to have some fringe benefits
and perks. We'd like to know who will be supervising us.
We'd like the security of being vested in a strong pension
plan. But economic conditions make this kind of control
increasingly unlikely.

In some ways this puts Christians in a similar position to the Israelites as they left Egypt and journeyed to
the Promised Land. They were totally dependent on
God for food and protection from their enemies. God
supplied meat and bread, but only on his terms. God
said, "Trust me. I'll give you what you need, but no more
than that."

No matter what the working conditions are on my
career path, 1 will still have to depend totally on God.
Knowing the details of the future is an illusion of inde-
pendence. I might as well learn to live dependently be-

cause that is reality, whether I'm comfortable with it or not. A healthy dependence is knowing and accepting God's provision on a daily basis. I can trust him totally to give me what I need for today. Tomorrow's needs will be met after I get my next night's sleep, not before.

*Lord, teach me to have a healthy dependence on you. Help me to be satisfied with what you have for me today. Help me to trust you for tomorrow's needs when tomorrow gets here and not be anxious beforehand.*

# Make an Accurate Assessment

*Do not think of yourself more highly than you ought,*
*but rather think of yourself with sober judgment, in*
*accordance with the measure of faith God has given*
*you. . . . We have different gifts, according to the grace*
*given us.*

*Romans 12:3, 6 NIV*

One of the best steps I took during my job change was to read Richard Bolles's book, *What Color Is Your Parachute?* As you go through the self-assessment process, he suggests that you need to identify the specific things you do well. He further suggests that most people are good at working with either people, information, or things. One of the exercises he advocates is an examination of your work history by listing all the jobs that you have ever held. Then you can go through that list and determine which three areas were your strongest. Where did you have your best successes? Where did you feel most inadequate? On which jobs did you get the most positive feedback from employers and fellow workers?

As I worked through this exercise, it didn't take me long to determine that my primary skill was working with information. I also learned that my people skills were worse than I had believed. The result of this process was that I went into a new information-oriented job with the confidence that I was in the right spot. I also became more conscious of my need to develop people skills because they did not come naturally to me.

The process was sobering, but it was also encouraging. It brought me down a couple of pegs in some ways, but it also boosted my optimism that I did have skills that were valuable.

When we lose a job and our self-confidence is shattered, it is scary to begin evaluating our strengths and weaknesses. I think we're afraid that our findings will cause us to lose the self-confidence we have left. Not so. Paul teaches clearly that God has given each of us special talents. Our job-changing goal must be to determine what those talents are and move in a direction that allows us to exercise them.

> How do you begin to improve your sense that you are in control, you are the steward or stewardess of your own life? You begin by inventorying your skills. Call them your gifts, your assets, your talents, or whatever. You need to inventory them, and then put them into some kind of prioritized order.
>
> RICHARD BOLLES, *WHAT COLOR IS YOUR PARACHUTE?*

*Father, when I go through moments where I don't know where my next measure of self-confidence will come from, give me courage to go through the process that can restore it. You've placed within me skills that are valuable. Help me to determine what they are so that I may truly serve you to the best of my ability.*

# Where Is My Stability?

*Truly my soul silently waits for God;*
*From Him comes my salvation.*
*He only is my rock and my salvation;*
*He is my defense;*
*I shall not be greatly moved.*
*Psalm 62:1–2 NKJV*

Futurists often talk about the rapid acceleration in the rate of change. Things change fast now, but they'll change even faster in the future! Job counselors now tell young people that they can expect to make seven or eight career shifts in their lifetimes. Technological advances and increased needs for information require that we learn more each year in order to do the same work. Younger people will continually come up through the ranks with more training. The ebb and flow of the economic and political climate means that we are increasingly affected by developments in various parts of the world. All these factors add up to an increased instability in our working lives.

As we think about our careers, we need to think through how we're going to respond to these kinds of circumstances. We need a mental and emotional framework to deal with probable career change and disruption. The Scriptures provide that structure.

While I can expect changes, I also can expect complete stability in God's character. This is the point of Psalm 62. I will always have a place to come back to. I can always expect his love to be the same. The way of ultimate salvation hasn't changed and will not. No matter what my circumstances, God will remain a shelter for me. Verses 11 and 12 point to God as loving and strong. He understands us, and he will carry out his promises to us. Even if virtually everything else in our lives changes, God will remain who he is for us.

*Remind me constantly, Lord, of the security I have in you. May you be that shelter that gives me the courage to deal with changes and circumstances I would prefer to avoid.*

# We Have More Resources
# Than We Think

*Not one of the men who saw my glory and the miraculous signs I performed in Egypt and in the desert . . . will ever see the land I promised.*
    Numbers 14:22–23 NIV, read Numbers 13–14

Why couldn't the Israelites learn from what God had done in the past? He had pulled them through several scrapes. He had supplied all the basic necessities of food, water, and shelter. He had given them protection, guidance, and military victory. His promises for the future were extensions of what he had already done. God asked the Israelites to go into unfamiliar territory, but with all the resources that he had demonstrated in Egypt and the wilderness. It was as if the Israelites were blind and deaf to what he had provided.

They aren't the only ones who couldn't see God's good provisions, though. How often are we unable to see the resources that we have available to us? We don't hear the promises of God. Our immediate fears freeze us. It's as if we were sitting in an apple orchard, starving but unwilling or unable to pick up a nearby ladder and use it to pick the apples.

The promises of God need to make a difference in how we look at our struggle. In the process, we must expect that he will stretch us beyond familiar territory into the unknown. While the process may not always be comfortable, the rewards are the fullness of the Promised Land as opposed to the dryness of the wilderness.

*Lord, help me to be flexible. Stretch me, even though it may be painful. Don't let me miss any opportunity that you have for me. Remind me constantly of the resources you give me and help me put them to use.*

# Security During Transition

*Why worry about clothes? Look how the wild flowers grow. They don't work hard to make their clothes. But I tell you that Solomon with all his wealth was not as well clothed as one of them.*
   *Matthew 6:28–29 CEV, read Matthew 6:28–34*

For the last several years we have vacationed at a little resort on a lake in northern Michigan. To get to the part of the lake that is good for serious swimming, you have to swim over a patch of weeds that are just below the surface. When I make that swim, the weeds seem to reach up and grab at my legs. Even though I know there's no real danger, I always feel uneasy as the weeds brush my body when I swim through them.

A lot of things that happen in a job change have the same kind of effect. Uncomfortable problems or circumstances lurk just below the surface. We have to get through them and we know we can, but they nag at us and give us a constant uneasy feeling.

Christ points us to the way to get through the problems: Seek his kingdom first. As I have to focus my physical energy on getting to a spot in the water beyond the weeds, so I need to focus my spiritual energy on the kingdom.

Christ teaches us that the only true certainty for tomorrow is God himself and his kingdom. The kingdom is the only thing that will last. We have to confess that many of our concerns are about those things that don't last. We have to work while trusting God, not our bosses, nor our customers. We have to learn to work knowing that what may be uncertainties to us are kingdom plans to him.

*Father, when all the nagging worries and concerns of this job change seem to immobilize me, remind me again to seek your kingdom first. Help me to want your kingdom even more than I want a new job.*

# Does Anyone Need
# or Want Me?

*You were saved by faith in God's kindness. This is*
*God's gift to you, and not anything you have done on*
*your own. It isn't something you have earned, so there*
*is nothing you can brag about.*

*Ephesians 2:8–9* CEV

We all have a desire to be wanted and needed in our work. Employers are often ambivalent about what they want their employees to feel. On one hand, bosses want their people to see themselves as being valuable to the company. On the other hand, they also want employees to know that no one is indispensable. The result is a nagging feeling of uneasiness that simmers in the back of our minds. We come to the point where we realize we're never going to get an unqualified yes to the question of whether or not we are wanted. Our worth to the company will always depend on how we perform. We always have to be prepared to answer the question "What have you done for me today?" It might not even be right to expect any more than that from employers. They also have the responsibility of surviving long-term. To abuse that responsibility would jeopardize the existence of a company and all its jobs anyway.

We can learn something of grace and love from this dilemma. Unlike employers' "concern" for us, God's love for us is unconditional. Our worth to God does not depend on our performance. It is determined by that love that caused Christ to die for us. He has provided for mistakes, failures, burnouts, and everything else that damages our performance. God can do that because his operation doesn't have to worry about going out of business or making a profit.

*Father, thank you for the depth and constancy of your love. May I take heart in the knowledge that you died for me. May that fact give me the security to step out in dependence on you.*

# Press On

*My friends, I don't feel that I have already arrived.*
*But I forget what is behind, and I struggle for what is*
*ahead. I run toward the goal, so that I can win the*
*prize of being called to heaven. This is the prize that*
*God offers because of what Christ Jesus has done.*
                                    *Philippians 3:13–14* CEV

When we leave a job, we often leave a part of ourselves.
We feel that we have worked hard at making things
work, often in less than ideal circumstances. We have
poured ourselves into people and projects, using up significant energy and effort. We may have had some major
accomplishments that deserve significant recognition.

While some people have the ability to walk away,
most of us, understandably, linger while we wonder what
we could have done differently. We replay in our minds
decisions we made or actions we took or didn't take.
Then we wonder, "Could I have done something to
change the current circumstances?"

While these emotions are deep and inevitable, they
can hurt us if we don't listen to Paul's counsel. Paul is single minded about moving ahead in Christ. He strains to
go forward. He has little regard for what he has accomplished. It isn't important anymore. There is no reward
in going back or in resting on laurels and praise, no matter how deserving. The only thing that really matters is
the prize of being obedient to the call of Christ. A run-
ner doesn't win a race by rejoicing in the ground that he

has covered. He wins by concentrating on getting to the finish line first.

*Lord, help me this day to focus on what you have called me to in the present and future. Help me to be proud of what I've done, but more interested in and motivated by what I have yet to do.*

# Stewardship Is Your
# Christian Advantage

> *So God created man in His own image; in the image*
> *of God He created him; male and female He created*
> *them. Then God blessed them, and God said to them,*
> *"Be fruitful and multiply; fill the earth and subdue it;*
> *have dominion over the fish of the sea, over the birds of*
> *the air, and over every living thing that moves on the*
> *earth."*
>
> Genesis 1:27–28 NKJV

When you are looking for a job, you can sometimes feel you're at a disadvantage in the workplace because you are a Christian. Your commitment to God does mean that you are unwilling to sacrifice body and soul for the company the way many employers want. On the other hand, there are some ways that Christians actually can have an advantage. They should have an excellent understanding of the nature of work, the nature of humans, and who the boss is. Together these can lead to a stronger identity and purer motivation. You can take on a new job with a renewed vision of who you are in God's creation

Genesis 1:27–28 points to work as stewardship—taking care of God's earth. If a Christian understands and applies the concept of stewardship to her work, she actually has an advantage in the workplace. She knows why she's there—to serve God. She has been created in the image of God, gifted with the ability to be responsible.

She carries out that responsibility to be a steward by exercising the administrative capabilities God has given her. She knows who she answers to ultimately. She knows who really owns all the company stock. She also understands that humans are fallen and therefore bent in much of their thinking. Sinful human nature will likely lead to some kind of grief in any job.

Does this understanding make work easier? Not particularly. Does it clear up confusing circumstances? Not always. It does mean though that I can get up every day with a renewed focus. The first line on our to do lists is always "Serve God Today." Because I carry that focus into my job, the details of my work fall into place.

If you demonstrate a strong sense of ownership toward your work, if you care about the way you perform, if you show your employers a high sense of responsibility, most of them are going to love having you as part of their work force.

*Father, thank you for creating me in your image. Thank you for what you have built into me. Thank you for creating in me a sense of stewardship. Help me to work as if each day was my first day on the job for you. Help me to make my understanding of your truth work for me. May I be your excellent steward in whatever task I do.*

# Christians Should Be
# Creative Employees

*Now the Lord God had formed out of the ground all
the beasts of the field and all the birds of the air. He
brought them to the man to see what he would name
them; and whatever the man called each living
creature, that was his name. So the man gave names to
all the livestock, the birds of the air and all the beasts
of the field.*

*Genesis 2:19–20*

Because we are created in the image of God, we are in-
herently "subcreators." J. R. R. Tolkien says "We make in
our measure, because we are made: and not only made,
but made in the image and likeness of a Maker."

As God's image bearers we all have gifts to be creative.
The ultimate creator of the universe designed us to be
creative. God expected Adam to be creative from the
very beginning. The first task given to Adam was that of
naming the animals. Sadly, most people have the mis-
taken notion that creativity is something that is the ex-
clusive domain of people involved in music, arts, and
crafts. People think it is a gift given to an elite group of
artists who write music or have booths at art fairs. Scripture teaches that creativity is also the domain of the pre-
schooler who makes Lego cars, and the homemaker who
juggles a myriad of daily responsibilities in the process of
making a home nurturing and hospitable.

Knowing that God has made creativity a part of us, we can have confidence that we can find creative solutions to problems in a work setting. We have enormous creative potential to develop ideas. Too often, though, we sell ourselves short. Don't ever label yourself "uncreative." Expect yourself to be creative. Expect yourself to come up with ideas to solve problems. Expect to see new and more efficient ways to get tasks done.

*Father, help us to better understand all of what it means to be created in the image of God. Help us to develop the creative gifts you've placed in us no matter what our job is or what we hear people say about creativity. Help us to see ourselves as you see us. May we be stewards of these gifts, producing fruit that honors you.*

# How to Deal with Worry

> *Do not be anxious about anything, but in everything,*
> *by prayer and petition, with thanksgiving, present your*
> *requests to God. And the peace of God, which*
> *transcends all understanding, will guard your hearts*
> *and your minds in Christ Jesus.*
>
> *Philippians 4:6–7 NIV*

There is no end to the ways we can worry while we're going through a job change. In fact, it is almost impossible
not to worry. We can worry about how old we are com-
pared to the job market, how long it will take to find another job, whether we'll find a job with conditions we
like, whether we'll have to move to another city for a
new job, what our true value is on the job market,
whether we can learn a whole new job again, and so on.
These kinds of worries seem to stand like water on a flat
roof looking for a hole or crack to get inside.

Paul's solution to worry is prayer. He acknowledges
the thoughts that go with being anxious, but he isn't
willing to let them dwell in his mind without praying
about them. He wants us to move quickly from worry to
petition. It makes sense. One of the reasons we often
continue to worry about a problem is that we seem unable to do much about it. By taking our needs to God,
we are doing something concrete. We also create an opportunity for God to answer.

*Lord, help my prayer to take on the regularity that demonstrates faith in your power to act in me and for me in these circumstances. Replace my tendencies to worry with a desire to pray. May the result of that prayer then be a new sense of expectation.*

# The "Joy" of Trials

> *Consider it pure joy, my brothers, whenever you face*
> *trials of many kinds, because you know that the testing*
> *of your faith develops perseverance. Perseverance must*
> *finish its work so that you may be mature and*
> *complete, not lacking anything.*
>
> *James 1:2–4 NIV*

Many of us typically react to this passage with something like "Easy for you to say," especially when we are going through a trial. *Joy* and *trials* seem to be like oil and water. When you put them together, there's a mess, and we would prefer to stay out of it.

James cleans up the "mess" by adding another word to the formula: *perseverance*. The three words are like three sides of a triangle. Then in the middle of the triangle is the idea of maturity. That is to say that God's plan for us is maturity. To become mature, we need to learn to persevere in trials. We also need to welcome this experience with joy because we realize that God uses trials to grow us up.

We easily forget that God is more interested in our inner character than he is on our position on the corporate ladder of success. What he wants for us is often substantially different from what we want for ourselves. We want resolution of trials. He wants us to be mature believers.

The great qualities of life usually come only when pain has begun, pain we may bring upon ourselves or pain brought by events and circumstances over which we have no control. When we fight the brokenness, or when we curse it as having no part of our existence, we forfeit the opportunity for quality growth.

GORDON MACDONALD,
*REBUILDING YOUR BROKEN WORLD*

*Lord, help me to realize that a life that is worth living is one that requires substantial amounts of perseverance to maintain and build relationships, to stick with reaching goals that are important, to mature into my potential. Lord, teach me to accept this process joyfully because your hand is in it.*

# The View from Pikes Peak

*Nothing about me is hidden from you!*
*I was secretly woven together deep in the earth below,*
*but with your own eyes you saw my body being formed.*
*Even before I was born,*
*you had written in your book*
*everything I would do.*

*Psalm 139:15–16* CEV

When tourists visit Pikes Peak, they learn (some for the first time) that the view from this mountain inspired the lyrics to the song "America the Beautiful." It's easy to see why. Being able to view hundreds of square miles in all directions at the same time gives a writer a vision far beyond what he could normally get with only a three- or four-mile horizon. Psalm 139 can give us that same kind of inspiring vision about our work.

Jobs sometimes contribute to a personal identity crisis. If we become too closely identified with our job, a change can cause us to suffer identity loss. If someone asks us who we are, do we answer with what we do? Are we primarily comfortable with ourselves only at work? Does our self-esteem take a mortal blow if a job doesn't work out as we'd hoped?

Psalm 139 gives us a bigger vision. It reminds us that our identities are tied to God. Our identities began long before the first job in our careers. They began at the point of conception. God was with us and knew us before we were even capable of thinking about a career. Further, he continues to sustain us, protect us, and know us just as well now as he did before we were born.

The more we understand these principles, the more we can relax about the future. The plan that was in place when we were conceived has not changed. God hasn't forgotten us. We need to make a career out of trusting God, knowing that he knows our needs and has promised to supply them.

> God will never allow any action against you that is not in accord with His will for you. And His will is always directed to our good.
>
> JERRY BRIDGES, *TRUSTING GOD*

*Father, it's scary to know that you know me better than I know myself. Because of that, though, I can trust you with the minutest details of my life. Increase my vision to see more ways that I can serve you through my work. Inspire me to be more fully the person you created me to be.*

# Renew Your Mind

*Therefore, I urge you, brothers, in view of God's mercy,*
*to offer your bodies as living sacrifices, holy and*
*pleasing to God—this is your spiritual act of worship.*
*Do not conform any longer to the pattern of this world,*
*but be transformed by the renewing of your mind.*
*Then you will be able to test and approve what God's*
*will is—his good, pleasing and perfect will.*

*Romans 12:1–2 NIV*

My pastor recently commented that the number one question that came up in his counseling sessions was "How do I find God's will in my career?" It isn't just the eighteen- to twenty-two-year-olds asking the question anymore. Our rapidly shifting economy has created situations where more people of all ages are wrestling with that question several times during their working lives.

Romans 12 says in effect that one finds God's will by having a "renewed mind." What does this mean for a time of changing jobs?

1. Distinguish between how God wants you to think and how corporate America thinks. Serving is appropriate. Aggressively climbing over people to get up the ladder isn't. As J. B. Phillips translates verse 2, "Don't let the world around you squeeze you into its own mould."

2. Trust God to meet your needs on a daily basis

instead of worrying about where your career will be in three years.
3. Think of yourself with sober judgment (verse 3). Become aware of your gifts and your weaknesses.
4. Make sure you're more concerned about who you are becoming than what you will be doing.

*Father, my mind is crowded with thoughts of the future of my career these days. I need your help in sorting it all out. Renew my mind daily by helping me to think as you would have me think. May my thoughts please you. Help me to see the way the world tends to squeeze my thinking into its mold. Help me to test all those thoughts against the standards laid out in Paul's letter to the Romans.*

# How Long, O Lord,
# How Long?

*Be merciful to me, LORD, for I am faint;*
*O LORD, heal me, for my bones are in agony.*
*My soul is in anguish.*
*How long, O LORD, how long?*
                                           *Psalm 6:2–3 NIV*

Whenever I hear the monthly unemployment figures, I'm reminded of the brief experience I had being laid off and collecting unemployment compensation. I remember that period as one of anxious waiting. Waiting often seems to dominate the process of a job change. We wait in lines. We wait for phone calls. We wait for a positive response through the mail. We wait for the newspaper or periodical with new listings in the want ads.

The wait is often particularly painful because we feel helpless in the process. When we talk with God about the wait, we don't often get satisfactory answers. The answer we want is an end to the wait. The answer we get is often to wait some more.

We can take some measure of comfort in the fact that the psalmists often felt the same frustration. They let God know how they felt. One of our comforts is that, like them, we too can express our frustration and pain to God. He isn't put off by our agonizing. He won't reject us because we complain to him.

Somehow the complaining makes room for God's

Spirit to provide an answer. Almost all these psalms of lament also conclude with the affirmation that God has heard the prayer and therefore the wait can be accepted.

As Thou wilt; what Thou wilt; when Thou wilt.
THOMAS À KEMPIS,
*IMITATION OF CHRIST*

*Father, I'm getting tired of waiting. I get frustrated feeling like I'm in limbo. Give me the patience to wait for your answer in your time. Help me again to believe your promises, even when I feel deserted. Hear my prayer and bring your will to pass.*

# A Job for Jonah

*But Nineveh has more than a hundred and twenty
thousand people who cannot tell their right hand from
their left, and many cattle as well. Should I not be
concerned about that great city?*

*Jonah 4:11 NIV, read Jonah 1–4*

Sometimes God calls us to do a job we don't want to do.
As in Jonah's case, the new job may require learning to
think differently or gaining new perspectives on our
well-established views of reality. While God had a definite role for Jonah to play in ministry to the city of Nineveh, he also wanted to change Jonah's way of thinking.
He wanted to expand Jonah's concept of his grace.

As Jonah did the job, God had him in a spot where
he could change his thinking. Jonah was forced to understand that God cared about the 120,000 people who
lived in Nineveh too. His grace extended beyond the
boundaries of Israel. From Jonah's prayer in chapter 2,
we understand that he knew God had power to act, as
opposed to an inactive idol. From chapter 4 we can see
that Jonah is forced to see that God acts internationally
and not just in Israel.

We can fight the job changes, or we can look forward
to them as new opportunities to learn. Like Jonah, I find
that I am often nearsighted about what God is doing. As
I look back at the various jobs I've had, I can see that in
each case I gained understanding into how people
thought and what motivated them. More often than

not, what I have learned has made me become a better person.

*Lord, help me to look forward to the opportunities to work with new people—to learn to know them and understand them, to minister to them to help extend the ministry of your grace.*

# Tongue Control During a Job Change

*Keep your tongue from evil,*
*And your lips from speaking deceit.*
*Psalm 34:13 NKJV*

Recently, a good friend of mine lost his teaching job after ten years in the same school. Subsequently, he interviewed with an acquaintance in a different state for another job. He failed to impress the interviewer because he spent a significant part of the conversation complaining about how he had not been appreciated in his previous position and how he was unjustly treated there.

Strong words come to the surface easily during a job change. Our tongues provide an outlet for expression of anger and frustration. We feel that it will hurt less if other people know about what happened. We look for sympathy anywhere we can get it.

We probably won't get it from prospective employers. Complaining should be confined to a couple of good friends and God. God won't be offended by it. He knows our need to vent. We see the psalmists doing it repeatedly. He has a ready ear for our inmost thoughts. Even the act of complaining to God puts us back in touch with him and his creative reality.

The way of prayer is not to cover our unlovely emotions so that they will appear respectable, but expose them so that they can be enlisted in the work of the kingdom.

EUGENE PETERSON,
*ANSWERING GOD*

*Father, thank you for being there to hear all my complaints. Thank you that I can cry out to you. It is comforting to know that you are not put off by my words of frustration. Thank you for listening and making me the beneficiary of your patience and love.*

# Finding the Right Fit

*And we know that all things work together for good to those who love God, to those who are the called according to His purpose.*

                                                    Romans 8:28 *NKJV*

One of the difficult aspects of changing jobs is having to figure out where one fits again. We're not sure of all the things that the new job may demand. In the old job we probably knew exactly where we fit and what was required. In a new position we're just not sure. We know we need to change, but we're not sure how or to what extent. We feel we're facing a series of question marks.

We got along with the job like that favorite suit we bought five years ago. It fits us well. We feel comfortable in it. We like how we look in it, but we have worn it so much that it is beginning to wear out. We'd rather keep it, but we can't. We have to find something new that will fit as well.

Maybe what we have to realize is that we need a higher view, that of Romans 8:28. Perhaps the higher our consciousness of God's plan for our lives, the less the specifics of what we are doing for work concerns us. Finding the right fit in a new job requires finding the right fit in God's overall plan. My first job is to trust.

To know that nothing hurts the godly, is a matter of comfort: but to be assured that all things which fall out shall co-operate for their good, that their

crosses shall be turned into blessings, that showers
of affliction water the withering root of their grace
and make it flourish more: this may fill their
hearts with joy till they run over.

THOMAS WATSON,

*A DIVINE CORDIAL*

*Father, don't let me forget your promises. Let the as-
surance of my salvation spill over into an assurance
of your plan for my life. May I grow in my trust of
what you have in store for me, not only in the world
to come, but also in this world.*

# Job Security

*Let us fear the LORD our God,*
*who gives autumn and spring rains in season,*
*who assures us of the regular weeks of harvest.*
  Jeremiah 5:24 NIV, read Jeremiah 5:20–31

When I finished my education and started my career, I had no security at all. As I look back I realize what enormous risks I took with a couple of those early job choices. At the time the jobs didn't seem risky to me because I didn't think I had much to lose. But now, fifteen to twenty years later, I don't even like thinking about the possibilities of job insecurity. I'm a little uncomfortable when there is talk of changes at work that may affect me. Any ideas that might mean losing what I've got make me squirm.

The current job market often puts us in situations where we're more like the farmers waiting for the rains to make their crops grow. It may be that we depend on God for employment the same way the Israelites depended on the spring and fall rains to assure their harvests. God controls the employment scene just as much as he controls nature. He is the Lord of the job market the same way he is Lord of the harvest. The best farmer in the world still depends on God for the rain. His security has to rest alone in God.

The word for us is to *fear* the Lord. It is he who assures us of our jobs. True job security is in knowing the ultimate Maker of all jobs.

*Lord, remind me every time it rains that jobs ulti-*
*mately come from you too. Remind me again of how*
*much I need to trust you and how graciously you*
*have provided in my past. Help me to see clearly how*
*you are the only true source of what I have.*

# Gaining Wisdom

*Do not forsake wisdom, and she will protect you;*
*love her, and she will watch over you.*
*Wisdom is supreme; therefore get wisdom.*
*Though it cost all you have, get understanding.*
Proverbs 4:6–7 NIV, read Proverbs 4

One of the ways to look at a job change is to see it as an opportunity to grow in wisdom and understanding. As the change takes place, you have an opportunity to step back and evaluate your performance. In this context, you'll probably be more objective about your abilities. A little distance can make strengths and weaknesses more visible. Your perspective may become clearer in three distinct areas.

First, you may see more of what God is doing in your life. Job changes help you to focus on your real priorities. They make you rethink God's call on your life. You can review how you got where you are and the assumptions you have had about God's plan for your life. Have you majored in the important things? Have you taken for granted that you can succeed on your own?

A job change also gives you a chance to look at how you're relating to people. Were you able to get along better in this job than the previous job you had? Did some of the same kinds of problems keep cropping up? Do you demonstrate more Christian character in your relationships now?

Third, a job change gives you the chance to ask questions about your own performance. Could you have done a better job of planning and organizing? Did you communicate with peers and superiors in a constructive manner? Did you adjust to the needs of your job in the context of a rapidly changing world?

As you or I go through this process, it works best if we do it with the perspective of the writer of Proverbs (4:11–12). Let the wisdom we gain guide us in the future, and we will not be hampered.

*Father, make me eager to apprentice myself to you. In a world where it seems people have a long list of things they want or need, may I put wisdom at the top of my list. I can survive financial difficulties. But wisdom is a commodity I can ill afford to be without.*

# Being Rich Toward God

*This is how it will be with anyone who stores up things for himself but is not rich toward God.*

*Luke 12:21 NIV*

Financial advisors tell us that we need at least six months' living expenses in the bank in order to survive a job change. Research indicates that a man commonly averages twenty weeks to find a new job, and a woman usually takes seventeen.

Scripture says that regardless of how much money we have, we are to be rich toward God. How do we do that when there's no money coming in and we're not sure when there will be? We can't help but feel that he needs to be rich toward us before we can be rich toward him.

Between jobs, we have time to think about how we've handled money in the past. Have our spending patterns honored God? Have we held on to every penny selfishly, or have we allowed God to work through us with the money he gave us in the first place? Do we love the gifts more than our generous Giver? Charlie Shedd had a formula that makes a lot of sense. He said, "Give 10 percent, save 10 percent, and spend the rest with joy and thanksgiving."

During a job crisis, we may not be able to give away or save very much money, but we can at least reorder our thinking. Christ points out that being prepared financially is more than having adequate money in the savings account. It involves having the right attitude toward

God. Our joy is only in relationship to our Lord. We can give thanks for his love and care. Only a fool doesn't see beyond his possessions.

Why not look at a job crisis as an opportunity to review your whole pattern of relating to money? Read a couple of books on the subject. Study some of the basic passages in Scripture that teach about money. Make sure you understand the basics and then apply them.

*Father, as I go through this transition, money is always at or near the top of my list of concerns. Use this time to shape my thinking so that I can be rich toward you. When I think about getting ahead, remind me that getting ahead with you comes first.*

# How High Are Your Expectations?

*Delight yourself also in the LORD,*
*And He shall give you the desires of your heart.*
                                    Psalm 37:4 NKJV

If you read reports of union negotiations, expectations are often the focal point of the story. The union expects higher wages, better benefits, or improved job security. Management expects improved productivity and better cooperation in a competitive business environment.

When we read through Psalm 37, our expectations of God are raised. It is full of promises that God will act on behalf of the righteous. We include ourselves in "the righteous" and assume these promises apply to our job circumstances. We can't understand when things go wrong.

But a closer reading indicates that we can expect things to go wrong. God never promised not to send famines and disasters on innocent people and prosperity to the wicked. As long as we live in a world where sin abounds, our jobs are at risk. The only part of life that is totally secure is our relationship with God. Everything else is temporary, including our jobs.

God never promised security in anything but himself. But what a wonderful gift he has given us! He himself is our security and our hope.

*Lord, thank you that your promises raise my expectations of you. I have every reason to expect deliverance. I know that when everything crumbles around me you are still a willing refuge. I praise you that I didn't have to negotiate to get these promises. You deliver on them by your grace.*

# Citizenship in Heaven

> *But we are citizens of heaven and are eagerly waiting for our Savior to come from there.*
>
> *Philippians 3:20 CEV,*
> *read Philippians 3:12–4:1*

Harvey Kuenn was an All-Star shortstop for the 1959 Detroit Tigers. That year he won the American League batting title with a .353 batting average. He later continued his career in baseball by becoming a manager. At one point, his job title with the Milwaukee Brewers was "interim manager," and a reporter ask him how he felt about working under those "interim" conditions. He answered, "In this business, we're all interim managers."

In his letter to the Philippians, Paul reminds us that our lives here are also "interim." The reality is that any job we have is a short-term or interim job. In 3:20 he reminds the Philippians and us that we are citizens of heaven. Above all else, we are God's people who are heading for a heavenly home. We may have excellent career prospects. Companies may want to sign us up for lifetime contracts. We may have fairly limited possibilities. We may be at an age or skill level where it's more difficult to even find a job. Whether we work in a job for thirty years or thirty days, it's still temporary to God. Either way, we need to maintain a focus on what it means to live for God rather than for a job or career.

One fact of reality . . . is that we are the pilgrim people of God. We are on our way home, but we are not there yet. We are only passing through this world.

JOHN POWELL,
*THE CHRISTIAN VISION*

*Forgive me, Lord, for the times when my work seems to take over my whole personality and vision for my life. Thank you for the reality of Paul's perspective. Remind me often that even a long-term career on earth is only a short-term prelude to heaven.*

# God Acts on My Behalf

*May the LORD answer you when you are in distress;*
*may the name of the God of Jacob protect you.*
                                        *Psalm 20:1 NIV*

When we go through a job change, we would all like to
have an attorney or an agent who would act on our behalf. If it could be someone from a prestigious law firm,
all the better. It would be a great confidence builder if
someone with a respected name and a detailed understanding of the issues was making sure we got the best
deal possible in a new job. It would reduce some of the
tension we feel to know that we had an advocate who
would thoroughly cover all the terms, conditions, and
benefits.

The message of Psalm 20 is that we have that kind of
help. God acts on our behalf. The chapter contains nine
different verbs detailing how God takes this action. He
answers, protects, sends help, supports, remembers, ac-
cepts, gives, makes plans succeed, and saves. We have the
best attorney available. Nothing gets by him. He remembers every detail of our lives and understands whatever circumstances we are in. One of his names is even
"Counselor." He stands alongside us in our most difficult times.

He anticipates every contingency that will come up.
He doesn't lose cases. His strategy has proven to be successful. He is always available, and there's already a permanent retainer in place. Jesus made the payment in full.

*Father, we easily forget how much you act on our behalf. Remind us when we're in distress that you are a God who listens and answers. Give us the wisdom to see and understand the answers when they come and patience to wait for the ones we don't have yet.*

# A Lesson from History

*I will open my mouth in a parable;*
*I will utter dark sayings of old,*
*Which we have heard and known,*
*And our fathers have told us.*
           Psalm 78:2–3 NKJV

A recent edition of *National Geographic* magazine had an article about the London Blitz in 1940. It was written by a man who was a teenager at the time of the bombing. Fifty years later he had gone back to reminisce on what had been his former life. His account is full of stories of people whose houses were replaced by bomb craters. Many of these same people were forced to begin new lives in new locations. He happened to be one of those who started over with nothing. He had since married, moved to Western Canada, and established a new home there. He was thankful that he had been spared in the destruction and was able to start over again.

Starting over with nothing can be part of God's plan too. While few of us want to be put in that position, it seems to be one of the more common experiences people have. So it was with Israel. They would have preferred a journey through the desert in a caravan of well-stocked motor homes. They thought it was enough just to be willing to go on the journey. Israel wanted to dictate the conditions of the journey.

God wanted them to accept the conditions of the journey because that was his way of teaching them to trust. His promise to supply their daily food and water would have developed the trust that he could also supply the essentials to win the military victories once they reached the Promised Land. Starting over can be an exciting and fruitful challenge when you accept God's conditions. On the other hand, it can be a fruitless and dry desert experience, if the whole process is accompanied by a desire to change the conditions.

*Lord, I admit I'm not fond of this idea of starting over with nothing. I'd rather start out with a full store of resources than to have to depend on you completely. Help me to reconcile my preferences with what you have to teach me. Help me to be a good student on the journey.*

# At the Mercy of the System

*Praise be to the LORD, who this day has not left you without a kinsman-redeemer.*

Ruth 4:14 NIV, read Ruth 1–4

One of the amazing aspects of Ruth's story is how much she put herself at the mercy of the Jewish system. She followed Naomi from her homeland of Moab back to Israel. Upon arriving in Israel she asked to go out and glean behind the harvesters, the acceptable way for the poor to gather food. She followed Naomi's instructions perfectly. She put herself completely at the mercy of the Hebrew kinsman-redeemer system in hopes that a kind relative would become her husband-redeemer. This "system" provided a means for a relative of a deceased man to marry the widow and carry on the family lineage.

The system proved to be friendly toward her. Even though she was a foreigner, she became a key ancestor in the lineage of David and Christ. God and his plan stood behind the social system.

When we're between jobs, we feel we are completely at the mercy of systems that aren't particularly friendly. It is difficult to understand the economic system we live in. We have almost no ability to change how it functions. The systems for finding jobs are too limited. Our complaints are similar to young job hunters who can't get hired because they need more experience and yet they can't get experience unless an employer hires them. They are at the mercy of a system that makes it difficult for them to break into the work force.

For the Christian, God's system is no less in place today than it was for Ruth. As Ruth found, his system is one of provision and protection. He is the ultimate Kinsman-Redeemer who knows the detail of my needs and provides solutions. He can rescue me from any danger or difficulty.

*Father, I'd rather solve my own problems. I don't like depending on someone else. I don't like being at the mercy of things beyond my control. Help me to relinquish those feelings in order to abandon myself to you. Help me to trust you as my Kinsman-Redeemer.*

# Feeling Sorry for Myself

> *The Israelites have rejected your covenant, broken down your altars, and put your prophets to death with the sword. I am the only one left, and now they are trying to kill me too.*
> *1 Kings 19:10 NIV, read 1Kings 19:9–13*

The Smothers Brothers have a routine where Tom makes the accusation that their mom loved Dick best. In the sketch, Tom recounts all kinds of silly reasons to support his contention. We all laugh because we know the whole argument is absurd.

My two sons often go into the same kind of routine (though not particularly comical) whenever there's conflict. One of them feels that he is getting fewer benefits or more discipline than the other. He feels sorry for himself and accuses my wife and me of loving the other one more.

I have to admit that, as parents, we occasionally get caught up in the argument and list all the reasons the boys are wrong. The whole conversation usually becomes somewhat silly. We love our sons very deeply. We feel confident about our sense of justice, and we understand that treating the boys a little differently is an acknowledgment of different personalities rather than lack of fairness.

As God's children, we sometimes regress to a childish mentality that makes a judgment on God's care when we feel mistreated. We feel sorry for ourselves because events aren't happening the way we expected. We want God to identify with us and tip the scales back in our favor.

After his experience on Mount Carmel, Elijah made such a complaint. He felt sorry for himself because he believed that he had done his job for God by confronting Ahab and the prophets of Baal. But the only result he saw was that after he had gone out on a limb for God, the queen put out a contract on his life. It just wasn't fair.

Did God get into a long, drawn-out argument with Elijah? No. Through a gentle whisper, he gave Elijah new direction and set him on course again.

*Father, I must confess that when things aren't going the way I would like, I'm prone to feeling sorry for myself. Help me to put aside those feelings. Open my ears to hear your comforting whisper that gives me encouragement. Help me to gain courage from the knowledge of what you have already done in me and will continue to do as you lead me toward maturity.*

# Half a Lifetime of Waiting

> *Then Samuel took the horn of oil and anointed him in*
> *the midst of his brothers; and the Spirit of the LORD*
> *came upon David from that day forward.*
>
> 1 Samuel 16:13 NKJV

When we get tired of waiting for a job, we can take some comfort from David's story. God assigned the job of king to David when he was a teenager. Yet, David didn't actually take over the job until he was probably in his thirties. No doubt, much of the agony David expressed in the Psalms has much to do with the struggle of waiting. The Director of Human Resources told him he had the job, and they would call back with his starting date. They didn't call for nearly twenty years. Not only that, but he spent those years taking care of sheep, running for his life, and hiding in caves. Maybe we don't have it so bad after all!

Understandably, we want to get into a job and do it now. We want to make our mark. We want to feel we're accomplishing great things. We want the financial security a job gives. We want the status that comes with being a well-employed, respected member of the community.

What God wants is to develop character in us no matter what job we're in. He wants us to learn to bear the fruit of the Spirit. He wants us to develop a mature relationship with himself. As with David, God wants us to develop a heart that seeks after him.

*Lord, when I get discouraged with waiting, remind me of David and his wait. Help me to use this waiting time to solidify my relationship with you. You have my attention. Teach me. I want to be your student. Develop in me the traits I need to serve you where you want me to serve.*

# Persistence Pays

*Won't God protect his chosen ones who pray to him day and night? Won't he be concerned for them?*
              *Luke 18:7 CEV, read Luke 18:1–8*

When I read this passage, I have little trouble believing it in my head. Then I have to admit that my prayer life is littered with prayers just as my teenagers' rooms are strewn with clothes just before cleanup day. Many requests I've tried once or twice and then abandoned. I've given up either because I didn't get an answer in the time frame I expected or I didn't want to be embarrassed by God's inability to answer the request. I worry that if I pray difficult prayers in front of my children, I won't be able to explain why God doesn't seem to answer.

Why do I have such a hard time being persistent? Why do I get so discouraged when I don't get an answer within twenty-four hours of a prayer request? Maybe I'm conditioned by TV programming where every mystery on the tube is solved in two hours. Every family problem has a neat resolution in thirty minutes. I don't know how to be persistent because I'm too conditioned to seeing everything resolved before I go to bed. I've got a TV mentality in my prayer life.

How can I change to the point where, like the widow in Luke 18, I'm actually inspired by the challenge of being persistent? By learning that what feels and looks like a wait for me may actually be God waiting for my personal prayer programming to change. While I'm programmed for quick resolutions to problems, he wants to change my life. While I want answers, he wants a relationship. Persistent prayer helps maintain that relationship.

*Father, thank you for the encouragement in this passage. Thank you that you not only provide answers, you also change the way I think. Remind me to be persistent when I feel like giving up. Keep me knocking on doors and making calls. Most of all, keep me coming back to you for the answers.*

# God Works for My Good

*For it is God who works in you to will and to act according to his good purpose.*

*Philippians 2:13 NIV*

Sometimes it's hard to believe that God is working out any good purpose in our lives. It feels as if we're just getting pushed around by arbitrary circumstances. We have to learn to believe the promise of Philippians 2:13 that God is acting in our lives. Whether we fully understand it or not, these circumstances will benefit us.

It helps if we take God's long-range view. He sees where we need to be ten years from now. God wants us to grow and will do whatever is necessary to see that growth happen. We forget too easily how short-sighted we are and how limited our horizons are as we look at our circumstances.

Changes are often setbacks, but they are also opportunities. A job change often means an opportunity to develop new skills, meet new people, acquire new knowledge, prove oneself in a new context. It is a chance to break out of stereotypes that may have been applied to us or roles that didn't make use of all of our abilities. It is a chance for God to move us in a new direction— one that may serve his purposes better, one that may prepare us for some ministry or bring us in contact with someone we may be able to help. You may even find five years from now that this change has been one of the best you have ever experienced.

*Lord, help me trust you when I can't understand what is going on. Help me believe the promise that you are working in my life and that your purpose for it is good. While I'm not always sure about the change, I am sure about you. Don't let me forget that fact.*

# Wasting Away

*Therefore we do not lose heart. Though outwardly we
are wasting away, yet inwardly we are being renewed
day by day. For our light and momentary troubles are
achieving for us an eternal glory that far outweighs
them all. So we fix our eyes not on what is seen, but on
what is unseen. For what is seen is temporary, but
what is unseen is eternal.*

*2 Corinthians 4:16–18 NIV*

The struggle of a job change sometimes makes us feel as
if we're wasting away. We feel that our idle skills are
growing rusty and brittle from lack of use. We can also
sense powerful emotional forces at work in us on the surface or just below it. Sometimes we have a measure of
control over them. Sometimes we don't. That wasting-
away feeling seems to have taken over our whole lives.
We feel like giving up. We think, *What's the use?* and lose
heart for the struggle.

Paul acknowledges the reality of those feelings in 2
Corinthians 4. They oppress us. They weigh us down
with a crushing burden. We are fragile creatures desper-
ately in need of a power beyond anything we can muster
from within. We need constant renewal in order to cope
with the issues and pressure that impinge on us.

Paul reminds us that there is a renewal process at
work in us even though we may not be conscious of it.
God doesn't let his people waste away. God's love,
through the comfort of the Holy Spirit, provides contin-

uous renewal in the midst of the deepest frustration. Our spiritual lives aren't like our bodies, which do deteriorate. For our whole lives we can trust God to energize us spiritually to cope with the most critical struggles.

Paul also encourages us to look to the glory that is our inheritance in God. He reminds us that our lives here are temporary, that what is to come is eternal. Thinking these kinds of thoughts while going through a job search may be virtually impossible all the time. But we need to keep coming back to them. God won't let us down in the larger scheme of things.

*Father, help me follow Paul's example. When I feel wasted and totally discouraged, remind me of the perpetual renewal process that is going on in me. May the energy of eternal life be infused in my body and soul today.*

# Noah's Wait

> *By the first day of the first month of Noah's six hundred and first year, the water had dried up from the earth. Noah then removed the covering from the ark and saw that the surface of the ground was dry.*
>
> *Genesis 8:13 NIV*

Ask any Sunday school veteran how many days it rained on the ark and you'll get an immediate answer: forty days and forty nights. Ask most seminary graduates how many days it took for the water to recede after the rain and you'll likely get a sheepish, blank look.

We don't hear much about Noah's thirteen months of waiting for the water to dry up. The Flood itself is the dramatic element in the story. The drying out process is only an interlude before the final sacrifice and promise of God.

We have visions of Noah's family huddled together as the storm beats down on the ark. We don't think as much about what must have been going through Noah's head in the year he waited to see something besides water, his family, and those smelly animals.

Waiting is part of God's culture. There's no avoiding it. There is only living with it. Sometimes God intervenes dramatically, and there is no wait. Other times he is content to let nature run its course. The wait probably accomplished something in Noah's soul. We can only speculate, but it likely made him appreciate God's promise all the more. Noah probably came out of the ark with a better relationship with God than he had when he went in. He built the ark out of faithful obedience. He survived the Flood with grateful thanksgiving.

I don't particularly like to wait. I don't like finding more than one person ahead of me at the check-out counter. I sometimes get anxious when the person ahead of me at the stoplight takes more than one second to start moving when the light turns green. I don't like having to wait for answers to prayer.

I'm also learning, though, if God says, "Wait," I don't have any more choice than Noah did. I do much better during the waiting process if I look for what I can learn rather than get anxious for the completed answer.

*Father, I need to understand how you work with people. I need to understand what you want to accomplish in and through me. Help me accept times of waiting as times of teaching. Help me look for what I can learn through waiting instead of just wanting the wait to be over.*

# It's Warfare Out There
# (and in Here)

*Nations surrounded me,*
*but I got rid of them by the power of the LORD.*
*They attacked from all sides,*
*but I got rid of them by the power of the LORD.*
*They swarmed around like bees,*
   *but by the power of the LORD I got rid of them*
   *and their fiery sting.*
         *Psalm 118:10–12 CEV, read Psalm 118*

In many ways, being unemployed puts one in an emotional and psychological battle. The enemy forces that surround us are dejection, discouragement, and despair. We feel that it's all we can do to defend the little bit of territory we have left, let alone go out and conquer new challenges.

A job loss rains torrents of dejection on us. A layoff or firing is like an explosion that blows us into the street. We're still intact, but shaky. Not feeling wanted or needed any longer leaves a crater in our self-esteem.

The problems with the national economy bring further discouragement. We see signs of downturns in most businesses that interest us. We have contacted all our friends and acquaintances who might have leads for us. Our phone calls go unanswered. Our letters and resumes get buried in personnel departments. We feel that our ship has sunk, and there is no rescue boat on the horizon.

Despair sets in when we feel we've used up our last ammunition and our food and water supplies are depleted. We feel completely surrounded by forces that have absolute control over us. We're about ready to give up the battle and surrender. We get to the point where a victory, a new job, seems increasingly unlikely. We seriously contemplate giving up the search.

It hardly seems time to begin a victory celebration, but that is exactly what the psalmist does when he gets to this point. In order to move from despair to celebration, he begins to recount the mighty acts of God. He reminds himself of God's character and how he makes himself a refuge, how he sets his people free, how his love endures forever, how he gives strength to weary people.

He is ready to lead a triumphant processional through the gates of the city. Groans of despair have been replaced by resounding shouts of victory because the mighty acts of God assure ultimate defeat of any enemy.

*Lord, it doesn't seem possible that the strength to defeat these emotional and psychological enemies is so readily available to me. Help me to recount your mighty acts in my life. Give me a vision of all that you have done in me and all you will do.*

# An Unexpected Answer

*But Naaman went away angry and said, "I thought
that he would surely come out to me and stand and
call on the name of the LORD his God, wave his hand
over the spot and cure me of my leprosy. Are not Abana
and Pharpar, the rivers of Damascus, better than any
of the waters of Israel? Couldn't I wash in them and be
cleansed?" So he turned and went off in a rage.*

*2 Kings 5:11–12 NIV, read 2 Kings 5*

Naaman was used to seeing events go as planned. After
all, he was the commander of the king of Aram's army.
When he gave his lieutenants orders, he naturally expected them to obey. When he designed a battle plan, he
expected his soldiers to carry it out. In fact, one of the
reasons for his military success was that he usually did a
superior job maintaining control of the battlefield. He
was able to dictate the outcome through planning and
preparation.

In the battle for Naaman's health, Elisha had to teach
him he was under a different set of rules—God's. Naaman had to learn the limits of his sphere of influence. He
had to find out that God didn't care what size army
Naaman commanded. God didn't read the papers to
learn and appreciate Naaman's battlefield statistics.

In a job loss we often go through similar ups and
downs. One day we have authority over our work and
how it gets done. The next day we don't have any work,
let alone any kind of authority. Instead of controlling the

destinies of a staff, we're controlled by outside forces, such as current hiring policies and industry conditions. God often uses these times of stress to teach us something, as he did with Naaman, because he has our full attention. He has something we want—an answer to our prayer for a job. His answer is that we must first be more attentive to him.

*Lord, you have my full attention. Whatever you want to teach me, I'm ready to hear. I'm eager to learn. Help me to unlearn preconceived notions that are of my own invention. Prepare me for the answers that you are going to give.*

# Rebuilding Your Self-Esteem

*You were rescued from the useless way of life that you
learned from your ancestors. But you know that you
were not rescued by such things as silver or gold that
don't last forever. You were rescued by the precious
blood of Christ, that spotless and innocent lamb.*

1 Peter 1:18–19 CEV

Three months after I lost my job, I remember telling
someone that I felt I had been stripped of all my self-
esteem. My perception was that my work had been of
significant value to the company. Losing my job meant
there were some, particularly those immediately above
me, who didn't see my worth in the same light.

When I tried to resolve those differences in opinion,
I was repeatedly told that they were right and I was
wrong. It was like baseball scoring. If the umpire calls
you out, you're out. It doesn't matter if you even have a
videotape to prove otherwise. If you don't agree, read the
box score the next day in the paper. The way he called it
is the way it is.

As I read Scripture I learned that I had a problem
when I based my self-esteem on what I thought I was doing for the company. When they took that market value
away from me, I didn't have much left. Getting my value
from an employment contract didn't work for long.

Peter points out that God places value on me for who
I am, not for what he can get from me. God established
my worth when Jesus died. No job loss can take that

from me. The company places value on me for what I can contribute to the bottom line. It's a business deal. God places value on me because he loves me. Love is its own bottom line. God says I have his love no matter how much I mess up. The cornerstone of rebuilding my self-esteem is God's love.

Your work matters to God. Your work has intrinsic value, because in it you mirror the God who is a worker, and who created you as His coworker. And your work has instrumental value, because it is one of the primary means by which you can love God, love others and love yourself.

DOUG SHERMAN,
*YOUR WORK MATTERS
TO GOD*

*Father, I know that through Jesus Christ you offer me a whole new way of life. May that "way" extend to my work life. Rebuild my self-esteem with the confidence that comes from knowing how much you love me.*

# Time on Your Hands

> *Trouble and anguish have overtaken me,*
> *Yet Your commandments are my delights.*
> *The righteousness of Your testimonies is everlasting;*
> *Give me understanding, and I shall live.*
>
> *Psalm 119:143–144 NKJV*

- A lamp
- A light
- Sweeter than honey
- Chief preservative
- Compass
- Strengthening agent
- Eternal life
- Love

These images of love for Scripture remind me of Elizabeth Barrett Browning's sonnet "How Do I Love Thee, Let Me Count the Ways." The psalmist has a love affair going with God's Word.

In these expressions, there is also a kind of feeling of leisure. It's as if Psalm 119 seems to be written by and for people with time on their hands. At 176 verses, it is the longest chapter in the Bible. It is an acrostic poem, which means that each stanza begins with a different letter in the Hebrew alphabet. The writer takes the time and space to affirm the value of God's law in every way imaginable.

While we're in a job crisis, we often have significant blocks of time available to us. The psalmist would clearly urge us to spend some of them in the Word. Let its comfort, direction, and power become a part of your life. Let the time that you have on your hands be a time of putting yourself in your Father's hands.

Only if we meditate on the Word of God, listen to God speaking to us, hear his voice and respond to him in worship, faith and obedience, will we grow into maturity in Christ.

JOHN STOTT, *GOD'S BOOK FOR GOD'S PEOPLE*

*God, help me to experience firsthand what your Word contains. Put a desire in me to learn from it. Make its teachings an inner daily guidebook rather than an external occasional reference work.*

# Constructive Thinking

*Finally, brothers, whatever is true, whatever is noble, whatever is right, whatever is pure, whatever is lovely, whatever is admirable—if anything is excellent or praiseworthy—think about such things. Whatever you have learned or received or heard from me, or seen in me—put it into practice. And the God of peace will be with you.*

*Philippians 4:8–9 NIV*

In the midst of a job crisis, thoughts often race through our minds like runners in the first mile of a marathon. Many of those thoughts are negative ones. What do you do about them? Think about it. What has your thought life been like in the last twenty-four hours? How well does the subject matter of your thoughts stack up against Paul's list here in verse 8?

It is no coincidence that this list comes after Paul's instructions to rejoice and pray. We all have difficulty maintaining that constancy of rejoicing and praying always. Many of our normal day-to-day activities keep pulling us off the rejoice-and-pray track. We know we're not going to be able to whip out a Bible and have a quiet time whenever we feel ourselves leaving the track. We can, however, be more active in dealing with the negative thoughts.

One of the exercises I found helpful in dealing with negative thoughts is to periodically write down and review a list of all the things I have going for me, internal and external. I remind myself of answers to prayer, of friends who have counseled me, of the things that have gone right. This activity puts a limit on my personal gripe sessions and often rekindles an expectant hope for the future.

The result of all this, Paul says, is that God's peace will be with us. While I may be prone to complaining, I have to admit that it does me little good. If I have a peaceful disposition, I know I'll be easier for everyone to live with, including myself.

> Never allow yourself to be pessimistic about your own state. Look outward instead of inward. And when you are inclined to be depressed and think you are getting on badly, make an act of thanksgiving instead, because others are getting on well. The object of your salvation is God's glory, not your happiness.
>
> LETTERS OF EVELYN UNDERHILL

*Father, help me to use my thinking time constructively. May it move me in directions that are positive rather than negative. May I honor you in thought as well as deed.*

# What Basket Are
# Your Eggs In?

*When Christ, who is your life, appears, then you also
will appear with him in glory.*

Colossians 3:4 NIV

Every time I read this passage, I marvel at Paul's concentrated focus on Christ. All of his eggs, so to speak, were in the Christ basket. Little else mattered to him. His anticipation of joining Christ in heaven was so complete, it was almost as if he had one foot there even as he wrote.

One of the issues that makes a job transition so tough is that we often put so many eggs in the job basket. Some of us get almost all of our self-esteem from our jobs. A career provides the primary challenge and motivating force in our lives. Jobs can also form a significant share of our social lives simply because of the large blocks of time we spend at them.

What would Paul say to all that? He'd ask, "Where is the body of Christ in your life? You think about developing a career. Are you also thinking about what you can do to develop relationships with people? What other kinds of service are you involved in? Have you given anyone a cup of cold water lately?"

The job basket won't bear the weight of our whole lives. It's too small and the handles aren't strong enough. The burden exceeds the capacity. The Christ basket, in contrast, has room for every part of our lives and is held together by the strength of heaven.

*Father, I'd like to echo Paul's prayer, but I'm not sure I can now. My eggs are pretty well attached to the work basket, and I'm afraid to move them because they're fragile and might break. Help me to understand what I can gain from a deeper relationship with you. Help me to trust you as I move toward a greater focus on living for you instead of for my job.*

# What Do I Say
# to the Kids?

> *These commandments that I give you today are to be*
> *upon your hearts. Impress them on your children. Talk*
> *about them when you sit at home and when you walk*
> *along the road, when you lie down and when you get*
> *up. Tie them as symbols on your hands and bind them*
> *on your foreheads. Write them on the doorframes of*
> *your houses and on your gates.*
>
> *Deuteronomy 6:6–9 NIV*

Michelle made a promise she couldn't keep. She had promised her eight-year-old daughter, Kerry, that she would pay for ballet lessons. The cost was ten dollars a week. Then came the announcement of the plant closing. She felt she had to take steps to eliminate all expenses that weren't critical for survival. The ballet lessons would have to wait, indefinitely. Kerry had a hard time understanding. Ten dollars a week didn't seem like much money to her. Every attempt at an explanation only ended in tears.

It is not hard to imagine that scenes similar to this one, described in a Detroit paper, are being played out in thousands of homes throughout the country. How can we expect young children to understand global economics and their impact on us? Our own government and our business communities are still struggling to understand what is happening and how to adjust for it.

There may be very little we can say directly that will help the children. There is, however, much that we can do that will indirectly help. Deuteronomy points to a whole way of life that interweaves God's teaching into family activities. Disasters and tough times are a part of human experience. Scripture doesn't attempt to hide that from us at all. In all those experiences, we see people struggle with their circumstances and still come back to the priority of loving and obeying God. To let your children share some in that struggle with you can only help them when they reach adulthood.

*Father, I'm frustrated that I can't give my children what they want. Help me to be satisfied that you can give them what they need. As I grow in my confidence toward you, may some of it also rub off on them.*

# Peace Under Pressure

> *I give you peace, the kind of peace that only I can give.*
> *It is not like the peace that this world can give. So*
> *don't be worried or afraid.*
>
> *John 14:27* CEV

To be peaceful in the middle of a job crisis seems to be humanly impossible. Who can feel peaceful about the possibilities of losing major assets? A few months of unemployment can wipe out home equity that took years to build. Any planning for the future has to be put on hold. How can we be peaceful when we have so little control over what will happen to us? It isn't humanly possible.

Interestingly, I think Jesus would agree. Peacefulness isn't generated out of our humanity. It is developed in us only as we learn it from God.

The world's image of peacefulness involves externals: a serene beach or pastoral scene, soft music, gentle breezes. It also expects immediate gratification and resolution to a problem. God gives peace by changing us from within, by making peace a part of our characters. He removes our fear of the unknown and replaces it with confidence in the One who controls all events. God puts peacefulness in us by changing us and how we think about our circumstances more than he changes our circumstances.

Verse 31 implies that this change to peacefulness takes place through a learning process. It isn't ingested like medicine that promises to be effective in an hour. It takes trial and error. It requires learning to give up well-entrenched ways of thinking. It demands growing in faith. It expects a commitment to discipleship. We learn peacefulness only by following closely after Christ.

*Father, forgive me when I want the benefits of your kingdom without paying the cost. Put a new desire in me to follow after you, to learn your ways, to become your disciple. Help me to see peacefulness, not as a cure to what is bothering me, but a result of my faith in you.*

# See Yourself as God Does

*Anyone who belongs to Christ is a new person. The
past is forgotten, and everything is new.*
                                    *2 Corinthians 5:17* CEV

Two months into my job crisis I had dinner with a se-
nior executive who was extremely proud of a younger
management team that had recently been put in place in
his company. The item that seemed to give him the most
pride was the fact that the recently hired team was all under age 40. I went to bed that night feeling glum. I had
just turned 42.

In a job crisis, events commonly happen that cause us
to see ourselves as having little value; as being washed
up; as incapable of accomplishing much worthwhile.

How do you see yourself? How does God see you?
What is the difference?

God sees us at our best: as people newly re-created in
his image; as forgiven and whole; as gifted and capable;
as individuals worthy enough to die for. He has a plan in
mind for us.

Being "in Christ" gives us a lot more than a place in
a pew on Sunday morning. It gives us a place in God's
kingdom. As such, we can be assured that God sees all
the potential we have. He doesn't write us off or put limits on us for arbitrary reasons.

If we can see ourselves as God does, we almost auto-
matically can grow in confidence. No matter where we

are in relationship to a job, we are still in the service of the king of the universe.

*Lord, sometimes I let circumstances or arbitrary and shallowly formed notions shape my opinion of myself. Help me to rise above those circumstances and opinions. Help me to see myself as you do. May the excitement I find in serving you carry over to whatever job I have.*

# The Friendship That Survives Any Crisis

*So let's come near to God with pure hearts and a confidence that comes from having faith. Let's keep our hearts pure, our consciences free from evil, and our bodies washed with clean water.*

*Hebrews 10:22 CEV*

Don't you question your friendship with people who only show up when they have a need of some kind? You wonder if you really are a friend or a meal ticket. You question the extent of your response. You are not even sure if you want to do anything to maintain the friendship.

These are also feelings we can project onto God. We can feel guilty about being in need and reluctant to go to him. We don't want to be the friend who only shows up when he's looking for a handout. Maybe we haven't done a very good job of maintaining a relationship with him, so going to him when we're in need seems rather tacky.

God says, "Come anyway." He is quite used to receiving people in our condition. Just as Christ's sacrifice broke down all barriers to the Jewish approach to the altar, so his death wipes out all the petty reasons we avoid coming to him. He has proven how much he wants our friendship. We can keep coming back even if we've virtually ignored him for a week, a month, or a year. His limitless love extends beyond what we can even imagine is possible. His friendship will transcend any crisis.

But the love of Jesus is utterly unaccountable—except that he is God and God is love. It has no cause in us. It reacts to, or repays, or rewards just nothing in us. It is beyond human measure, beyond human comprehension. It takes my breath away.

WALTER WANGERIN, JR.,
*RELIVING THE PASSION*

*Thank you, Jesus, for providing a friendship that thrives in crises. Help me to turn readily to you with no hesitation. You are utterly dependable. You gave your life to preserve the relationship. Praise you, Lord.*

# Knowing Where to Get Answers

*Praise be to the name of God for ever and ever;*
*wisdom and power are his. . . .*
*He gives wisdom to the wise*
*and knowledge to the discerning.*
*He reveals deep and hidden things;*
*he knows what lies in darkness,*
*and light dwells with him.*
   Daniel 2:20–22 NIV; read Daniel 1–2

How many times have you asked yourself the following kinds of questions in the last few weeks: What am I going to do? Who should I talk to? How many resumes should I send out? What do I need to do to prepare myself?

If a kind of miracle happens today and someone calls you with an acceptable job offer, that's great. More than likely though, you're going to have to make decisions and answer some of those questions by taking action.

The royal astrologers complained in Daniel 2:11 that the king's request to interpret the dream was impossible because the gods "do not live among men." Daniel knew differently, and so do we. Daniel knew wisdom was available from the God who created us and lives among us. When he needed the wisdom to interpret the king's dream, he knew exactly who to ask for it. He prayed for the wisdom. He expected it. And he told the king in no uncertain terms about his source of wisdom (2:27).

Wisdom is similarly available to us. God has promised. We have twenty-four-hour access. He also has twenty-four-hour access to our minds. There are no guarantees that you will become a master dream interpreter, but you can accept the firm assurance that God will guide you. You are not alone as you make decisions. God can give you the wisdom to understand yourself and wisdom to understand the companies you may be researching.

*Father, there's nobody here that provides better answers than you do. When I flounder in the deep water of questions that seem to have few answers, throw me the life preserver of your wisdom. Help me to grab on and then pull me to shore.*

# Does God Know What He's Doing?

*Before him all the nations are as nothing;*
*they are regarded by him as worthless*
*and less than nothing. . . .*
*Do you not know?*
*Have you not heard?*
*The LORD is the everlasting God,*
*the Creator of the ends of the earth.*
*He will not grow tired or weary,*
*and his understanding no one can fathom.*
    Isaiah 40:17, 28 NIV; read Isaiah 40

My all-time favorite movie is *Chariots of Fire*. One of my favorite scenes in the movie takes place when Eric Liddel, the great Scottish sprinter, is preaching on a Sunday morning in Paris during the Olympic foot races. The passage he reads for his sermon is this one from Isaiah. While he is reading, the movie cuts to races that are taking place at the Olympic track simultaneously. While nation competes against nation to prove athletic superiority, Liddel points out that God says all nations have little future. God controls the destinies of rulers and politicians and public figures, no matter how much power they think they have.

When times are rough, we wonder if God is really in charge. We wonder why he lets us get jerked around by so many economic and political forces beyond our control. We wonder if he really even cares whether we have a job. If he really is in charge, does he know what he is doing?

The testimony of Isaiah is a resounding *Yes!* Nations may rise and fall. Rulers may come and go. God remains both Starter and Finisher. What we see and mostly live with are temporary conditions in the scheme of eternity. As God sustains the stars in heaven and the whole universe, he sustains our lives. We may not be able to say that every day, but if we keep coming back to him, he will not disappoint us.

*Help me to tune in to what you are creating in and around me, God. Help me to be aware of what is permanent and what is temporary. Remind me that while economic and political conditions change, you don't.*

# Joseph and the Technicolor Job Crisis

> *Joseph had a dream, and when he told it to his brothers, they hated him all the more. He said to them, "Listen to this dream I had: We were binding sheaves of grain out in the field when suddenly my sheaf rose and stood upright, while your sheaves gathered around mine and bowed down to it."*
>
> *Genesis 37:5–7 NIV*

Who could call Joseph's career path anything but remarkable? He had to go through a maze of obstacles that would have boxed in most of us permanently. His career included betrayal, rejection, neglect, and finally success. He experienced serious setbacks and disappointments that should have left him devastated. It is hard to imagine a career that included all that happened to him.

Joseph started out at the absolute bottom as a slave, made good progress, was thrown back to the bottom, and yet still rose to the top of an empire. He grew from being a pampered little boy to a position that controlled the destinies of hundreds of thousands. We would be hard pressed to find a better example of a godly response to a job crisis.

Take the extra time to read through the entire story (chapters 37, 39–48 in Genesis). It is one of the most richly textured in Scripture. It has all the features of a typical TV miniseries: family jealousy, sexual aggression, and political intrigue. As you read, look for what Joseph had to do to succeed. Try to identify with him and feel some of what he must have felt. You may feel that you've been treated just as unfairly as Joseph. But God has not abandoned you. He brought Joseph through his trials, and he will help you too.

*Thank you, God, for Joseph's story. Help me to see the principles in it. Help me to apply them to my crisis. Help me to grow in resiliency as Joseph did. Encourage me through your inspired word to see more than just the crisis. Help me to see what I can learn from it that will make me a better employee.*

# Deal Constructively with Disappointment

> *The LORD was with Joseph, and he was a successful man; and he was in the house of his master the Egyptian.*
>
> *Genesis 39:2 NKJV*

The first verses of Genesis 39 read like a story out of *Business Success* magazine. Joseph was given the reins of Potiphar's household businesses. He immediately turned them around and made them prosper. He gained Potiphar's complete trust with all the possessions, including the land. Scripture makes it clear, though, that it was not just Joseph's expertise and hard work that brought about success. Several times, the Lord is mentioned as the source of his prosperity. The text goes to great lengths to say that the Lord was with Joseph. Even after Joseph was thrown into prison, it says the Lord was with Joseph there. With the Lord's help, Joseph was even able to make the prison function better.

It is hard to believe that Joseph felt he was having success in either of these situations. It seems more likely that he felt a profound sense of disappointment. He had performed well. He had helped his superiors prosper, yet he was stuck in a jail cell.

Even in disappointments, God is with us. It may not be easy to accept the fact that God's idea of a successful career is not a climb up a corporate ladder. No matter what rung we are on, his purposes are accomplished and we can fit into his plan.

Any kind of work will make a difference in "how things turn out." And to the Christian, the way God wants things to turn out is what life is all about.

PHYLLIS TAUFEN AND
MARIANNE WILKINSON,
*LOVING YOUR WORK EVER AFTER*

*Father, sometimes the feelings of disappointment surround me like an early morning fog. I don't want to move out and do much of anything because I'm afraid of all the things I can't see. Help me anticipate the clearing off of this fog. Help me move to be in a good position when the visibility improves.*

# Learn to Accept
# God's Timing

*Now a young Hebrew was there with us, a servant of the captain of the guard. We told him our dreams, and he interpreted them for us, giving each man the interpretation of his dream. And things turned out exactly as he interpreted them to us.*

Genesis 41:12–13 NIV, read Genesis 41

How often do you get annoyed because the traffic lights aren't timed correctly? How often do you get frustrated because the weather turns out to be lousy when you have an outdoor event planned? How often do you get frustrated when God's timing on your career development is different from what you would like it to be?

One of the more difficult lessons for us to learn is that God's timing is not like ours. His whole view of time is different. If we stop and think about it, having an eternal view does make our shortsightedness look quite inadequate. We can't afford to get frustrated with God's timing and let it negatively affect our relationship with him or the most important people in our lives.

Joseph spent years in jail waiting for an opportunity to prove himself. When that chance came, he was ready to accept responsibility for the entire nation of Egypt. God used those years in Joseph's life to develop him for an enormous task. We shouldn't be surprised if we don't get immediate answers to prayer. God's agenda may well be different from ours. What we should be concerned about is developing character—the kinds of traits that prepared Joseph to do the job when he had the opportunity. We see in him patience, endurance, foresight, discernment, closeness to God, the ability to trust God in the middle of suffering.

> Joseph named his firstborn Manasseh and said, "It is because God has made me forget all my trouble. . . ." The second son he named Ephraim and said, "It is because God has made me fruitful in the land of my suffering."
>
> GENESIS 41:51–52 NIV

*Lord, forgive me for thinking that events need to revolve around me and my perceived needs. Make me willing to do your bidding and not only accept what happens, but accept your timing on the events in my life.*

# Cultivate an Attitude
# of Service

> *So the warden put Joseph in charge of all those held in*
> *the prison, and he was made responsible for all that*
> *was done there.*
>
> Genesis 39:22 NIV, read Genesis 39–41

In one infamous transaction, Joseph's brothers stripped him of his robe, his privileged position in his family, his heritage, and his identity. He went to Egypt with nothing. Yet, in a few short years, he established himself as a capable steward of Potiphar's household business. So much so that he could say that his master had entrusted everything to his care (39:9).

When Potiphar's wife made her false accusation against Joseph, he ended up back at the bottom again, in prison. The same developments occurred in confinement. Over time Joseph became the steward of the jail house. This position in turn led to the relationship with the butler, who later introduced Joseph to Pharaoh. Joseph found favor with the men who were over him because he carried out the role of the servant. Even though he deserved better, he accepted his position and fulfilled it well.

As you go through the struggle of transition in finding a new job, ask yourself several questions this narrative raises: How do you feel about being a servant? Do you see yourself fitting into the role of a steward? Are you content to stay in that role or do you see it only as a stepping-stone to get to a position of higher authority? Does the idea of stewardship motivate you or turn you off?

At each step of his career,

Joseph gave no sign of seeking the number one position. Rather he sought only the best interests of the person in charge. He wanted what was best for everyone involved.

GORDON MACDONALD,
*FACING TURBULENT TIMES*

*Heavenly Father, give me a heart that truly does seek after the best interests of others. Help me to accept the role of a servant graciously and even eagerly. May I learn to be a steward that brings honor to those I serve.*

# Become a Problem Solver

*The seven years of abundance in Egypt came to an end, and the seven years of famine began, just as Joseph had said. There was famine in all the other lands, but in the whole land of Egypt there was food.*

*Genesis 41:53–54 NIV*

Joseph succeeded where many of us fail because he was a problem solver. He had success under Potiphar, under the jailer, and under Pharaoh because he made things run better and he correctly anticipated the future.

We can appreciate what Joseph did. In a time of apparent prosperity he forced what must have been an unprecedented level of frugality on the people. That would be political suicide these days. Our politicians can't seem to be frugal even in times of serious recession. But Joseph was able to keep the country on course over a period of years when nobody else anticipated the coming problems. There must have been people asking Pharaoh what he was letting this "foreigner" do.

He also ably managed the rationing in the times of famine. He made the supplies, built up over seven years of plenty, last for the entire seven years of famine. He shrewdly used food to extend Egypt's influence internationally. God gave Joseph a vision, and he stuck with it. No doubt, having that vision helped him when his popularity suffered or when people didn't appreciate what he was doing to prepare for the future.

Ask God to give you a vision of what you can accomplish. Begin with the immediate task you have of finding a new job. What has God been preparing you to do? See the task of getting a new job as a healthy challenge, a problem to be solved.

*Lord, infuse me with excitement about what I can accomplish. Help me to look forward eagerly to solving problems rather than shying away from them. Give me a willingness and stick-to-it-iveness to respond to the challenges I face. Let me begin today.*

# Remember That God Has
# a Job for You to Do

*And now, do not be distressed and do not be angry*
*with yourselves for selling me here, because it was to*
*save lives that God sent me ahead of you.*
                                              *Genesis 45:5 NIV*

Everybody says hindsight is 20/20. Joseph demonstrated
that to his brothers toward the end of his story in Genesis. What I wonder is, Did he have that clear a vision of
what God was preparing him to do while the preparation
was taking place? Probably not. I doubt that his trek from
Palestine to Egypt was filled with eager expectation at the
opportunity to join the political scene there. It's also hard
to imagine that his first few days after being imprisoned
by Potiphar were filled with thoughts of ways to improve
the living conditions of the Egyptians. Questions surely
must have come to his mind when the butler promptly
forgot him after Joseph had predicted his good fortune.

Joseph must have had some sense of destiny, though,
because he was clearly able to get on top of each setback
he experienced. In each instance we read the phrase
"God was with him." We ask, *What does that mean?*
*What was that like?* Gordon MacDonald puts it well. He
says that what Joseph had was a sense of destiny that is a

quality born with the human spirit, conceived
there by the Holy Spirit of God. It is a quality

which instinctively discerns conditions and circumstances, determines appropriate responses and directs through word and deed the efforts of people toward the superior alternative.

*FACING TURBULENT TIMES*

*Father, help me to develop that sense of destiny in my own life. Give me a job to do that provides a place for me to help further your kingdom. From that sense, may I have the fortitude to make it through difficult times.*

# Adapt Willingly to God's Plan

> *So then, it was not you who sent me here, but God. He made me father to Pharaoh, lord of his entire household and ruler of all Egypt.*
>
> Genesis 45:8 NIV, read Genesis 45:1–15

I'm always amazed when I read about Joseph's graciousness in dealing with his siblings, who sold him into slavery expecting never to see him again. Understandably, the brothers could have expected Joseph to seek revenge. Joseph had to reassure them repeatedly that he had their best interests at heart. They were justifiably afraid that he would use his power and position to take revenge.

It is interesting that many of us find it easier to identify with the brothers than with Joseph. We understand their reaction. We have a harder time understanding Joseph's. His ability to see all his years of obscurity and frustration as part of God's plan is a model that stretches us to see our circumstances in different ways.

Nobody in their right mind would have *wanted* to follow the career path that Joseph did. He was forced to leave his family, his home, his inheritance, his language, and his identity. He understood that God's purposes are more important than our desires for comfort and security. Joseph didn't just endure; he adapted to his circumstances and was successful even in the face of several devastating setbacks.

The happiest and most successful people are those who are fleet-footed, who are eager to learn new ways, who adapt to new systems when the old ones do not work.

ALAN LOY MCGINNIS,
*THE POWER OF OPTIMISM*

*In all the changing circumstances we face, grant us, Lord, the ability to adapt. Help us to focus on whom we serve instead of the inconveniences and differences that can discourage us.*

# God Specializes in Fresh Starts

> *In that day I will restore*
> *David's fallen tent.*
> *I will repair its broken places,*
> *restore its ruins,*
> *and build it as it used to be.*
> *Amos 9:11 NIV*

Our family moved several times when I was a child. I particularly remember that one of those moves gave me a fresh start in my sophomore year in high school. I was no longer a marked target for certain bullies. In the new school, girls didn't know me as a nerd. Athletic coaches didn't write me off as the awkward one. I had a chance to build a new reputation without any of the baggage from younger days.

So it is with a new job. A new job gives us the opportunity to leave behind negative evaluations, difficult relationships, and pigeonholes that may have boxed us into limited or predictable behavior.

How can we make the most of the new start? How can we convert nervous energy into productive motivation? What are the keys to changing our worry into calm assurance and confidence?

Again the Scriptures give us helpful examples and principles. A fresh start is one of the central benefits of establishing a relationship with God. The prophets all point to a bright new future as a result of turning to God. Paul talks about becoming a whole new creation when we start fresh with God. Nobody is better at giving new beginnings. We need to learn personally the depth of his grace, the breadth of his power, and the life-changing dynamics he introduces into our work habits and attitudes.

We can even think of the Bible as a preamble to our new employee manual. As Paul says, the Bible is helpful "for resetting the direction of a man's life. . . . The scriptures are the comprehensive equipment of the man of God, and fit him fully for all branches of his work" (2 Timothy 3:16–17 PHILLIPS).

*Thank you, Father, that you never tire of giving me fresh starts. Your patience is infinite. Your understanding is comprehensive. I know that with the guidance of the Holy Spirit and the instruction of your Word, I have the resources available to take on any new task. Keep me in touch with you and those resources.*

# Confidence

> *But Moses said to God, "Who am I that I should go to Pharaoh, and that I should bring the children of Israel out of Egypt?" So He said, "I will certainly be with you. And this shall be a sign to you that I have sent you: When you have brought the people out of Egypt, you shall serve God on this mountain."*
>
> Exodus 3:11–12 NKJV, read Exodus 3–4

One would have thought that Moses would be happy when God called him to leave the backside of the desert. He had been raised in Pharaoh's court as a prince and ended up a sheepherder in Midian, many miles from Egypt. Instead, Moses resisted on every point he could imagine. He was full of "what ifs" and "I can'ts." He looked for every conceivable reason to avoid taking on a new job. Even after he started back to Egypt, he still must have been objecting because Exodus 4:24 says God almost killed him!

Either he must have been scared for his life, or he had settled into a comfortable middle-aged pattern and didn't want it disturbed. He lacked confidence in God and in God's ability to work through him. He had to be taught that:

- God has already thought of all the contingencies.
- God provides all the tools you need to get the job done.

• It's dangerous and foolish to resist God's call on
  your life.

Are these lessons that you need to learn too?

*Father, if I have been in a rut and not living up to
my potential in serving you, move me out of it. Make
me pliable to get on board with your plans and not
resist change just because it is disruptive and somewhat scary. Give me a desire to do the best and be the
best at whatever you have planned for my life.*

# When a Job Change
# Requires Relocation

*Then a teacher of the law came to him and said,*
*"Teacher, I will follow you wherever you go."*
  *Jesus replied, "Foxes have holes and birds of the air*
*have nests, but the Son of Man has no place to lay his*
*head."*

                                        *Matthew 8:19–20 NIV*

If you have to move to start a new job, you will experience a double load of stress. The two areas of upheaval are often braided together in a way that ties us in knots. Most of us aren't comfortable with the nomadic way of life and all the uncertainties that go with it. Let's face it: We probably weren't brought up to be pilgrims. While a job may only be one part of our lives, having to relocate to take on a new one disrupts almost every other part.

Jesus' words to the lawyer seem somewhat harsh. After all, the man was at least expressing a serious desire to follow Christ. He said he would follow Christ anywhere he went. Jesus could have acknowledged the inquiry and thanked him for it. He must have known, though, that the lawyer wasn't willing to accept all the conditions that went with following.

When God calls us to move, it can be helpful to switch into a pilgrim mode. You can abandon yourself to God in a way that may be unfamiliar at first, but may lead to a healthier relationship with him. You can put yourself in a position to experience a new level of dependence on God. You can get a taste for a relationship that is unencumbered by many of our normal cares. Ask yourself, *What would happen if all you could take with you was what you could carry in one suitcase?*

There is no thrill like the way of Christ, and there is no glory like the end of that way; but Jesus never said it was an easy way. The way to glory always involved a cross.

WILLIAM BARCLAY, *THE GOSPEL OF MATTHEW, VOLUME 1*

*Father, while I may not particularly look forward to moving, help me to look forward to the opportunity to follow you. If I have no place to lay my pillow down, I know I can lay my head on your chest. I am never really homeless as long as you're with me.*

# Forced to Rebuild

*And he moved from there and dug another well, and they did not quarrel over it. So he called its name Rehoboth, because he said, "For now the LORD has made room for us, and we shall be fruitful in the land."*

*Genesis 26:22 NKJV, read Genesis 26:12–34*

It is not too hard to imagine the kind of frustration Isaac's servants felt as they dug the third well. When the first wells were dug, their sore backs and blistered hands had little time to heal before they were told to abandon them, move, and start digging all over again. They probably expected to be able to drink the water from them for at least the next couple of years. Instead, they had to walk away without being able to enjoy any benefits from their work.

Few of us enjoy that prospect of rebuilding from scratch when we move for a new job. We dread church shopping, dealing with the utility companies, getting all our identification changed to the new address, watching our kids struggle to build new friendships, trying to reestablish a support system.

In the midst of all the moving and well-digging, what happened to Isaac should also be a lesson to us. Isaac was finally able to settle more permanently. In this process, God was able to remind Isaac again of the promise he had made to Abraham's family. Every time they moved, they were able to find water again. The disruptions of a move don't last forever. God's promise for protection, resources, and a future with him continue to be fulfilled even when we feel exhausted, scared, and frustrated all at the same time.

*Father, help me see the rebuilding as an opportunity to look forward to, not a burden to be dreaded. Give me energy to cope with all the varied and difficult circumstances that accompany a move. May I even derive some joy from being on the course that you have set.*

# Leaving the Support
# System Behind

> *How great is your goodness,*
> *which you have stored up for those who fear you,*
> *which you bestow in the sight of men*
> *on those who take refuge in you.*
> *In the shelter of your presence you hide them*
> *from the intrigues of men;*
> *in your dwelling you keep them safe*
> *from the strife of tongues.*
>
> Psalm 31:19–20 NIV

One of the hardest parts of moving to take a new job is leaving behind one's support system. We usually spend years building up that system. Experiences and relationships interact to give us a network of friends that we trust, friends who know and accept us. These are the people we go to when we need to talk through something. These are the people we can ask to help us with projects and circumstances when we lack resources.

In a move, our need for support increases even though the resources are usually less. We're like a quarterback whose blocking has broken down. Pressures are mounting, and we feel we have nowhere to turn. What can we do?

David's response to these kinds of pressures was to see God as his support system. He trusts in God's goodness. He knows that God has resources David can use. He knows that God is a refuge in times of stress. He also knows that God expects us to come to him when we have these times of crisis. We can be strong and have hope because we have God's sustaining love. We can "take heart" because God has put the resources of heaven at our disposal. He preserves the faithful.

> God is good, He is goodness itself. Goodness is not a measuring rod applicable to everything, including God Himself: it is but another name for God Himself.

ROMANO GUARDINI,
*THE LAST THINGS*

*Produce in me, Lord, this same faith that David had. Help me to be willing to come to you and let you supply me from the goodness of your storehouse of love.*

# Questioning the Wisdom of Relocating for a Job

*The Lord had said to Abram, "Leave your country, your people and your father's household and go to the land I will show you."*

*Genesis 12:1 NIV, read Genesis 12–22*

Many of us assume that when we feel called to make a move for a new job, the subsequent process of the move should be relatively smooth. We're surprised when Murphy's Law comes into play. House sales fall through. Lawyers delay the negotiation process. Banks get bogged down in paperwork. We find unexpected mechanical problems in the new house. The kids have trouble adjusting to new schools or making friends.

Interestingly, though, an expectation of a smooth move doesn't have much biblical precedence. Look at the life of Abraham. After God called Abraham to move, the biblical story tells of one problem after another. First, Abraham experiences famine and has to go to Egypt. Then, after a family quarrel, Abraham and Lot go separate ways. There is military conflict. Sarah's barrenness leads to an awkward family lineage. Finally, God puts Abraham through a severe test on Mount Moriah.

We're shortsighted. We forget that God's purposes have eternal implications, and he will carry those out in ways that may not conform to our expectations. Also, he has a process of maturity in mind for us. In that process, the Bible tells us we can expect trials and difficulties.

*Father God, help me to look beyond the immediate inconveniences and see more of what you have for us. Help me to remember that you didn't promise to make the way wide and smooth, but you did promise to be with us. May I take great comfort in that.*

# Wanting to Go Back to Egypt

> *They said to Moses, "Was it because there were no graves in Egypt that you brought us to the desert to die? What have you done to us by bringing us out of Egypt? Didn't we say to you in Egypt, 'Leave us alone; let us serve the Egyptians'? It would have been better for us to serve the Egyptians than to die in the desert!" Moses answered the people, "Do not be afraid. Stand firm and you will see the deliverance the LORD will bring you today. The Egyptians you see today you will never see again. The LORD will fight for you; you need only to be still."*
>
> *Exodus 14:11–14 NIV; also read Exodus 17:3; Exodus 16:1–4; and Numbers 14:1–4*

On at least four different occasions, the Israelites asked to go back to Egypt. It seems they wanted to turn tail and run from every difficulty they faced. When we read of the Israelites' desire to go back to Egypt, our reaction is almost one of incredulity. We ask, "How could they be so stupid? Why would they want to go back to slavery? Couldn't they believe that what was ahead of them was better than what was behind them? Couldn't they understand that where they were going to was better than where they were coming from?"

God asked the Israelites to risk their future with him, and they were deaf to his promise and blind to the actions he took on their behalf. Because of their deafness and blindness, a whole generation lost the opportunity to move into the Promised Land.

Moves are risky. We can suffer enormous material and relational loss. We need to see these difficulties as temporary or momentary setbacks. When God moves us out, he has in mind a place to go. We can see a move as a call. God may put a new group of neighbors in front of us who need a helpful friend. He may have a church where our gifts are needed. He may use the move as a way for us to grow spiritually.

The promises of God always include deliverance, protection, and sustenance. When God asks us to move, the resources to make the move come with the directions.

*Lord, when I feel discouraged at the moving process, remind me that the Scriptures give me directions to go through the process. Help me not to let the intensity of the workload cause me to lose track of where the directions are.*

# Motivation

*So Jacob served seven years to get Rachel, but they seemed like only a few days to him because of his love for her.*

*Genesis 29:20 NIV, read Genesis 29:16–30*

The first lesson to learn from this passage is be careful about working for your future father-in-law, especially if he has two daughters he wants to marry off. The second is that the right motivation makes it possible to work in all kinds of circumstances. Verse 20 gives us a picture of a young man whose motivation completely controls his attitude toward his work.

Jacob was able to put up with some pretty lousy working conditions because he was motivated by his love for Rachel. In fact, the text says that the motivation was so strong that it made the years of working seem like "a few days."

One of the things many of us need to cultivate is our own sense of motivation. If, as the Westminster Catechism says, the chief end of man is to glorify God, then we need to grow in our understanding of how we do that at work. A job transition gives us an opportunity to re-examine our motives. Money and status are basic but often short-lived. To glorify God in work is to work to please him by serving, not by trying to "get ahead."

The church of Christ does not need smug professionals, preoccupied with managing their own careers. The church does not need success-oriented members who reach out only to other winners. The church does not need those who expect the good life because of how hard they work. Instead, Christians are to live out the original ideal of the professions: to serve rather than to be served.

NATHAN HATCH, "PERILS OF
PROFESSIONALISM,"
*CHRISTIANITY TODAY*,
11 NOV. 1991

*Father, I'm sure that a lot of my motives haven't always been to serve others or even you. My tendency is to serve myself first. Help me to see specific patterns that need to improve. Give me a sense of purpose in what I'm doing that is inspired by the fact that I'm a part of your kingdom.*

# Who's the Boss?

*Whatever you do, work at it with all your heart, as
working for the Lord, not for men, since you know
that you will receive an inheritance from the Lord as a
reward. It is the Lord Christ you are serving.*

*Colossians 3:23–24 NIV*

We all know the difference a good or bad boss can make
in a job. A good boss can make a mediocre job enjoyable,
and a bad boss can make a good job miserable. As we
look for a new job or start one, we want to look for situations where we can learn from our bosses, where we
know we will be treated fairly, and where we will have
opportunities to advance. While we all want to have a
good boss, we know that we're likely to get some bosses
that aren't so great at times. At those times it is critical
that we remember who is really the boss: God.

Paul's teaching on work implies that no matter what
we do to earn a living, no matter who supervises us, the
real Boss, the One we ultimately answer to is God. He
understands all that we put into a job. He knows every
detail of every bit of work that we do. He appreciates us
when it seems that no one else does.

Working to please God means that when the times of
change and stress come, we have more of that relationship with him to fall back on. Current circumstances
have less influence on us because we realize if God is the
boss, he is also in charge. He promises not to give us
more than we can endure. He promises that all things

will work together for our good. With these kinds of promises coming from the real Boss, I can work in circumstances that are less than ideal.

Who is the boss? God is. I work for him.
Work not to become a saint but to give glory to
    God.

SOURCE UNKNOWN

*Father, I thank you that you are my Boss. First and foremost, I report to you. By your Holy Spirit, remind me when I forget that you're in charge.*

# Go in the Strength You Have

> *The LORD turned to him and said, "Go in the strength you have and save Israel out of Midian's hand. Am I not sending you?"*
>
> *Judges 6:14 NIV*

Management consultants say that one of the qualities of a good leader is that he or she is able to get people to do more than they think they can. He stretches people. She gets them to find abilities they didn't know they had. He inspires them to take on challenges that seem beyond possibility.

Scripture confirms this pattern. Repeatedly, the Bible recounts stories of individuals who take on new battles or missions and perform better than anyone could have expected. Moses, Joshua, Deborah, David, Elijah, and the disciples were all led by God to take on jobs that could only be done in God's strength.

In the time of the Judges, defeating the Midianites looked to be a challenge beyond the capabilities of the Israelites. It certainly seemed beyond Gideon, whose claim to shame was that he was the "least" in his family of one of the weakest clans in the smallest tribe (verse 15).

But Gideon succeeded because he obeyed God and went with the strength he had, which was God's strength. He was instrumental in defeating the Midianites because he was willing to let God stretch him and infuse him with divine strength. This strength is evident in Gideon's trust, in his courage and bravery.

As you work to find a new job, or when you start one and find yourself confronting self-doubt, remember you have more strength than you think you have. Go with it.

*Father, I need to submit to your leadership. I know you're going to stretch me, and I don't like being stretched. It is uncomfortable and painful. Remind me that you have a clearer vision of where I should be going. You know better than I what I can become. You know what you can accomplish through me.*

# When You Feel Your Job Is Second Best

> *For I have learned to be content whatever the circumstances. I know what it is to be in need, and I know what it is to have plenty. I have learned the secret of being content in any and every situation.*
> *Philippians 4:11–12 NIV*

For years my wife has kept a card above our kitchen sink that contains the message "Contentment is not the fulfillment of what you want, but the realization of how much you already have."

I find that I have to relearn this lesson all too frequently. Notice that in Philippians, Paul says he has "learned." This lesson didn't come in an overnight revelation, but through the fire of experience. One could make a case that there is no other way to learn contentment than going through tough times. Hunger normally is not a vicarious experience. We have to go without food ourselves to learn to be content while hungry.

Paul doesn't say it's easy, only that it can be done through Christ's strength. Contentment isn't some inner resource that we develop to the point where it becomes a part of our character. It is more a by-product of depending on Christ for our lives.

There will always be a lure of bigger income, the possibility of a better boss, or the opportunity for better working or living conditions. We don't want to cut ourselves off from those choices, but we do want to make them in a context of contentment. Sometimes being content may even mean that relocating for a new job is the wrong decision.

*Father, there are internal and external forces that often leave me with feelings of discontent. Help me to sort them out with the strength you give me. Help me to see the lure of "bigger and better" for what it is. Help me not to shy away from what I have to learn in order to make use of the strength you put in me.*

# Stretching

*The voice spoke to him a second time, "Do not call
anything impure that God has made clean."*
                                    Acts 10:15 NIV, read Acts 10

Acts 10 records an intriguing account of one of the
major steps on Peter's career move from fisherman to
apostle. God had to get into Peter's brain, rewrite the
programming, and override a lifetime thought pattern.

The pattern was that Jews didn't associate with Gentiles. In particular, they didn't eat with them because the
"pagans" were unclean. For Peter to be effective in his
new job, he had to learn a new attitude toward Gentiles.
Rather than write them off or shut them out, he needed
to learn to issue the invitation to receive the gospel
openly. Jesus died to save them too. His grace was meant
for Jew and Gentile alike.

Not all the Christian community learned that lesson
so easily (see Acts 15). These life-long thought patterns
linger in the stew of their own failures. They drag a
forward-looking venture into the past. God intervened
dramatically, through a dream, to teach Peter a new way
of thinking. He stretched his mind to prepare him for a
cross-cultural ministry that would change the course of
world history.

What thought patterns of yours does God want to
change? Do you put people in boxes? Do you make
room for them to grow and mature? Are you happy

when those around you succeed? Are your expectations too limited? It may be time to reprogram your thoughts.

*Father, help me to examine thought patterns and prejudices that affect me at work. Root out those that harm me and the people I work with. Correct my nearsightedness. Give me a vision to see people and the world more as you do. Stretch me to be a better person for other people to work with.*

# Growing Up on the Job

> *When I was a child, I spoke as a child, I understood as a child, I thought as a child; but when I became a man, I put away childish things.*
>
> *1 Corinthians 13:11 NKJV*

An integral part of raising children is accepting and living with childish immaturity. How else can our kids grow up? Most of them will exhibit behavior that we parents hope is limited to the stage they are in. Some of that behavior includes a lack of mouth control: loudness, being overly critical, whining and complaining, preoccupation with self, lack of responsibility, inadequate follow-through.

Next question: Have *you* been guilty of any of these behaviors in your recent jobs? I have to confess that I have been guilty at work of many things that irritate me when I see them in my children. I may be a little more subtle, but the effect is just the same.

Most of the problems I cause originate with my tongue. I say things that are better left unsaid. I say things that put other people down in order to puff myself up. I complain about ownership and management decisions before I understand all the circumstances.

Sometimes I'm reluctant to take responsibility for my own failures. I don't own up when I goofed. I work harder at making sure someone else gets the blame than correcting my share of the mistake. I get carried away with doing projects I like and neglect doing the things that would make other people's jobs easier or better.

I need to be sure I've grown up on the job. I need to speak like an adult, with wisdom and discernment. I need to concentrate on the tasks that further the goals of the company rather than my private interests. I need to accept full responsibility for the quantity and quality of my work.

*Lord, help me to see the childish ways in my own behavior at work. Help me then to put those behaviors behind me. Bring me to new levels of maturity that are only possible as I become more fully identified with your Son.*

# The Thankful Minority

*When one of them discovered that he was healed, he*
*came back, shouting praises to God.*
                    *Luke 17:15 CEV, read Luke 17:11–19*

Did you ever do something extra for someone and he or
she never bothered to thank you? The lack of thanks
doesn't do much for the relationship. In fact, it can leave
a hole in the relationship that may need serious repair.

It's hard for us to imagine the dramatic change that
healing brought to a leper's life. The healing would have
allowed him to physically be near people again. Severe
restrictions about where he could walk and live would
have been lifted. There may have even been a regenera-
tion of toes and fingers that had been lost because of the
disease. Healing gave him a future with opportunities instead of only pain and death. Yet only one of the ten
healed lepers bothered to return to Jesus and give thanks.

We can get caught up in the challenge of a new job
and forget God's hand in it. We can attribute our success
in finding a new job to our own hard work and ingenu-
ity. Sometimes we have prayed for something so long
that when God answers the prayer, we respond with "It's
about time," rather than with heartfelt thanks.

Thanksgiving is an implicit part of faith. In the
Samaritan leper's case, his act of thanksgiving signaled
the establishment of a relationship with Christ. The nine
who failed to give thanks missed out on knowing Jesus
and maybe even on the spiritual healing that could have

gone with the physical. Paul even goes further to say that the failure to give thanks is ultimately destructive.

> For although they knew God, they neither
> glorified him as God nor gave thanks to him, but
> their thinking became futile and their foolish
> hearts were darkened.

ROMANS 1:21 NIV

*Merciful and gracious God, count me with the one leper who returned. I, too, fall at your feet praising and thanking you. Any success I have, I attribute to what you've done in me and for me. I'm blessed to know you care about me and the details of my life. May I bring glory to your name through my work.*

# Where Is Your Heart Leading You?

> *"You acted foolishly," Samuel said. "You have not kept the command the LORD your God gave you; if you had, he would have established your kingdom over Israel for all time. But now your kingdom will not endure; the LORD has sought out a man after his own heart and appointed him leader of his people."*
> *1 Samuel 13:13–14 NIV, read 1 Samuel 13*

Why did Saul fail where David succeeded? In many ways their backgrounds and experiences were similar. Both were chosen by God out of rural obscurity. Both were prone to experience emotional highs and lows. Both won favor with the people by being militarily successful. Both were called on the carpet by a prophet for their sin. So what is the difference? Why did God fire Saul and hire David?

David chose to seek after God's heart. Saul chose to follow his own heart into folly. Saul thought more of his own ideas than he did of God's. Then when he was corrected, he failed to repent. He got his annual review, was told he wasn't making it, and still proceeded to act as if he could win God's favor without obeying God's commands.

When you start a new job and motivation is running high, you can forget who got you there in the first place. The desire to succeed can take over. You can slip into a pattern of focusing all your energies on impressing your new employer. You can virtually let the job take over your life. Time on the job can squeeze out both God and family.

The day you start the new job, put a monitor on your heart. Keep checking it. Ask a friend to check it too. The way to healthy job tenure is through the spiritual health of your heart.

*Father, I know you want me to succeed in my work. I also know that real success cannot come at a cost of my relationship with you. When urges toward self-preservation begin to take over, help me to work harder at maintaining my relationship with you.*

# New Feelings About
# Old Hurts

> *If you forgive others for the wrongs they do to you, your Father in heaven will forgive you. But if you don't forgive others, your Father will not forgive your sins.*
> Matthew 6:14–15 CEV

Most of us have a propensity to remember old hurts. Our abilities to practice forgiveness are often limited by at least one or two grudges. We may even hold a special grudge against someone who *caused* us to lose our job. We can get a kind of perverse pleasure in hanging onto old hurts. We store them up like snowballs in the freezer to pull them out in the summer and be able to hurl them at the one who hurt us unexpectedly.

Christ's words on forgiveness, from the Sermon on the Mount, could hardly be more explicit. Get rid of the snowballs. Put them out in the sunshine and let them melt. God doesn't treat you that way. You cannot afford to treat former employers that way either.

Think some new thoughts about old jobs. What did you learn? Who did you meet that you've had a positive, lasting relationship with? What skills did you gain? How did the job help prepare you for new experiences? Few jobs are a total waste.

Think some new thoughts about former employers. Have you forgiven their lack of understanding? Can you forgive their callousness and arbitrariness? Can you put behind you any wrong you may have suffered?

> It is forgiveness that supplies the healing scream of the long-term tomorrows. For long distance, forgiving is stronger than hate.
>
> LEWIS SMEDES, *FORGIVE AND FORGET*

*Jesus, I confess my tendency to hold grudges. I know they aren't doing me any good, but I still hang on to them. Help me to take to heart your words. Put a new spirit within me, a spirit of forgiveness. You set the best possible example. Help me to follow it.*

# Crossing the Jordan

*And as soon as the priests who carry the ark of the LORD—the Lord of all the earth—set foot in the Jordan, its waters flowing downstream will be cut off and stand up in a heap.*

Joshua 3:13 NIV, read Joshua 3

For a whole generation, the Jordan River stood as a physical and symbolic barrier to the Promised Land. The Israelites didn't have enough faith. They didn't think they could conquer the inhabitants of the land. They preferred the dry safety of the desert to the wet danger of crossing into the unknown. They died without experiencing what could have been theirs. The promises of the new land went unfulfilled, not because God couldn't make good on his promises, but because the Israelites were unwilling to do what God commanded.

Are you conscious of any barriers that may be keeping you from going to a new job with the right attitude? Are you stepping out with the right kind of God-trusting aggressiveness? Like the Promised Land, the new job is there to be conquered. Timidity is no asset when you walk in the door for the first time. The job won't begin to be conquered until you cross that threshold.

Identify the crossing point and ask God to give you the courage and faith to step out at that point. Even look forward to the obstacles you will face as opportunities for God to prove his promises. You may have a whole new exciting career ahead of you, but you won't find it until you make the crossing.

> God gives us a specific promise in the Bible for every problem. . . . We have a Lord who not only helps us grow through our problems, but gives us the power to triumph over them.
>
> LLOYD JOHN OGILVIE, *IF GOD CARES, WHY DO I STILL HAVE PROBLEMS?*

*Father, I thank you for being a God of promises. You give them. You fulfill them. I don't want to miss any that are meant for me. Give me enough faith to experience the fullness of your faithfulness.*

# God's Standards of Professionalism

> *They could find no corruption in him, because he was trustworthy and neither corrupt nor negligent. Finally these men said, "We will never find any basis for charges against this man Daniel unless it has something to do with the law of his God."*
>
> Daniel 6:4–5 NIV, read Daniel 6

As you make a fresh start, you want to be known as a professional. You want to be seen as someone who approaches work with excellent skill and good judgment. You want to get the job done in a way that pleases customers, superiors, and staff.

Daniel built that kind of reputation in a political arena that was probably full of corruption and intrigue. The fact that he was a paragon of professionalism didn't keep him out of trouble. Darkness doesn't want the light to shine on it.

The first and primary rule that formed Daniel's professional standards was "Always obey God's commands first." His primary relationship was with God. King Darius—his boss—came second. Upon hearing the decree to pray only to the king, Daniel went home and immediately prayed to God, just as he always had. There was no hesitation. Obedience took precedence.

We probably won't face the same kind of dilemma that Daniel did. The ones we face are more subtle. We can get so involved with getting our careers back on track that we forget which track we should be on. We think we are only in a temporary phase that will get under control in just a few weeks. Then two years later we find that there's significant distance between us and our families, or us and God. Sunday school legitimately makes Daniel a hero for kids. Let's make him a hero for us as adults too.

*Father, no matter what I do, I want to be known as a professional. As I develop my skills further, help me to maintain the right standards of obedience to you. Help me to understand the subtle pressures that would undermine that obedience. Rather than be consumed by work, let me be consumed by my love for your commands.*

# Redefining Success

*. . . that we may live peaceful and quiet lives in all
godliness and holiness. This is good, and pleases God
our Savior, who wants all men to be saved and to come
to a knowledge of the truth.*

1 Timothy 2:2–3 NIV

What is your image of a successful person? More often
than not, it is probably a Type A personality. A "successful" person is usually aggressive, hard driving, always
moving, the first in the office in the morning, and the
last to leave at night. Often he or she is consumed by a
frantic kind of busyness and motivated by strong forces
to get ahead.

Scripture projects a different image of success. It suggests that to be successful in pleasing God, we need to be
Type G and H people: Godly and Holy. The world often defines success by position, wealth, and power. God
defines it in the context of obedience, discipleship, and
faithfulness.

An inability to be a Type A person doesn't constitute
failure in God's economy. God wants you to be consumed by him, not by your work. The way to success is
not a corporate ladder. Rather it is through a relationship
with Christ. In that relationship God wants us to live his
way of life, his commands integrated into our daily activities.

As you make another fresh start, what are you doing
about building that relationship with Christ? How are

you going to balance work and non-work activities?
How are you going to get yourself on a discipleship track
as well as a career track?

I do not pray for success. I pray for faithfulness.
MOTHER TERESA OF CALCUTTA

*Father, I feel I don't know very much about being
godly and holy. Teach me. Help me to know the success that comes from following you unreservedly. May
my goals be ones that honor you, and may I achieve
them through means that glorify you.*

# Faith Is More Important
# Than My Job

*In this you greatly rejoice, though now for a little while you may have had to suffer grief in all kinds of trials. These have come so that your faith—of greater worth than gold, which perishes even though refined by fire—may be proved genuine and may result in praise, glory and honor when Jesus Christ is revealed.*

*1 Peter 1:6–7 NIV, read 1 Peter 1:3–10*

In the letters of Peter there are groups of principles that have a great bearing on the workplace. They apply easily to a job change because they were written to help people who were going through tough times. As you understand and apply these principles, you'll be able to step back and gain a better perspective on your career.

The first and most obvious principle is that one's faith is more important than any job. If someone asked me about my priorities, I would certainly give this idea a lot of lip service. But I'm not sure how much I let it make a difference in my attitude toward work. Peter speaks of our hope being in Christ. All too often my hope is in the size of my raise next year or in the possibility of a promotion.

I have to confess that I'm largely earthbound, thinking about the next ten to twenty years rather than an eternity with Jesus. I worry that my retirement plans are not adequate when God has the best inheritance waiting for me in heaven, and there I'm fully vested. I worry about job security and about where my job can take me. I wonder about job satisfaction. I ask too much of the job and not enough of Christ.

In chapter 1, Peter pulls us back quickly to the reality of priorities. Too easily we regard our jobs as our lives. While this is understandable, given the time and energy we put into our work, it falls far short of what God intends. God wants my work to proceed out of the context of my faith. The reality is that I usually live with my faith sandwiched in between my work and leisure. Career isn't a basic building block; faith is. And the career decisions need to proceed from my faith commitment.

*Father, as I go about the process of rebuilding my career, help me to see it in the context of my faith. Help me to focus on my career in a way that pleases you, not ignores you. May my cultivated faith make for a fruitful job.*

# Faith Is the Context
# for Working Hard

> *Therefore, prepare your minds for action; be self-controlled; set your hope fully on the grace to be given you when Jesus Christ is revealed.*
>
> *1 Peter 1:13 NIV, read 1 Peter 1:13–25*

- Be prepared for action.
- Be self-controlled.
- Set your hope on grace.
- Do not conform to evil desires.
- Be holy.
- Live your lives as strangers here in reverent fear.

If Peter were writing an employee manual, he might use this passage as a preface. While Peter teaches that our faith is more important than our work, he also teaches that our faith provides a context for our work.

These imperatives throughout the passage appear to be a curious blend of things that we should do now and ideas we should carry out in the future. At first glance these seem to oppose each other. Some are very much oriented to the here and now, the others toward the there and then. Any employer would put the first two phrases into an employee manual. Few would include the rest. They sound too pie-in-the-sky.

The conclusion is that God wants us to live with that tension—working as hard as we can today while looking forward to the day when our work here is done. We live in the time between D Day and V-E Day. Like the successful Allied landing at Normandy in 1944, Christ's death and resurrection signify the ultimate final victory. We work to help complete what he started. We redeem the time by working in the context of his victory over the grave.

Do we work less hard because God has it all under control and the victory is assured? No, we work all the harder because we want to bring his victory to completion and bring him glory in the process. Martin Luther said, "If I knew the Lord was going to return tomorrow, I would plant an apple tree today."

*Father, help me to have the same attitude as Martin Luther. May your present and future glorification give me motivation to work hard at my job. Help me to keep my nose to the grindstone as I look beyond it toward you.*

# Faith Security Is Better
# Than Job Security

> *But you are a chosen people, a royal priesthood, a holy*
> *nation, a people belonging to God, that you may*
> *declare the praises of him who called you out of*
> *darkness into his wonderful light. Once you were not a*
> *people, but now you are the people of God.*
> 1 Peter 2:9–10 NIV, read 1 Peter 2:1–11

Almost every Wall Street Journal or newspaper business section these days has some report of companies that are merging. Computer makers are deciding they need to join forces because the competition with each other has eroded profit margins to precariously small levels. Banks and other financial institutions are buying each other to dominate market shares. Auto manufacturers are continually striving for an international perspective that will allow them to produce the same parts and cars for several different countries. The most common result of all of these moves is to cut the headcount.

Evidence is ample that we are in an economic era where companies can and will rise and fall with remarkable rapidity. Mergers and buyouts will be daily occurrences. Keeping a resume up-to-date may need to be a fairly regular rather than an occasional task. Most young people will see more layoffs and job changes in their careers than their parents could have imagined.

While our faith won't protect us from being caught in

the middle of those changes, it does give us a tremendous framework of identity to see us through the changes. Faith gives us an identity with God and with other Christians that will be there when jobs are eliminated, companies go bankrupt, and the rungs on the corporate ladder break. If I understand that I'm a part of the "people of God," "a holy nation," "a royal priesthood," I wear an ID badge that gives me eternal life security rather than job security.

> He is no fool who gives up what he cannot keep
> to gain what he cannot lose.

JIM ELLIOT, *SHADOW*
*OF THE ALMIGHTY*

*Remind me always, Father, that my strongest points of identity are with you and your family and not with my job. No matter where I work, no matter what I do to make a living, I will still be a part of your holy nation. May that give me comfort and confidence to work so that you may be glorified through my work.*

# Work Respectfully
## as unto God

*Submit yourselves for the Lord's sake to every authority instituted among men.*
1 Peter 2:13 NIV, read 1 Peter 2:13–25

As a baby boomer who attended college and graduate school in the late '60s and early '70s, I sometimes have difficulty obeying this command in 1 Peter. During those years, I picked up some tendencies toward cynicism that are still with me. I sometimes bristle over decisions that seem wrong to me. I'm not good at "working unto God" when what I'm asked to do doesn't make sense.

But God doesn't ask me to understand my employers' decisions, just to treat them with respect and give them my best work. I have to appreciate the responsibilities my superiors have, the burdens they shoulder, the balancing acts they have to perform for employees, customers, and owners. And not only do my employers have a bigger picture than I do, but God has a bigger picture than they do.

The reason I can work under human authorities in my job is that they aren't my real employers. Ultimately I answer to God. In a sense I'm on loan to my company, much as a worker from a temporary employment agency. I know I'm on my way to a completely different kind of career in the City of God.

The person in authority has the responsibility, is accountable, is compensated and will have to answer for his decisions. He has the right to be wrong.

JERRY JENKINS, *TWELVE THINGS
I WANT MY CHILDREN
TO REMEMBER FOREVER*

*Lord, I'm pleased to be a part of your work force. Help me to bring glory to you no matter what job I'm doing today. Help me to accept the authority that is over me now because ultimately I know that you gave it.*

# Expect the Best from God

> *And the God of all grace, who called you to his eternal glory in Christ, after you have suffered a little while, will himself restore you and make you strong, firm and steadfast.*
>
> 1 Peter 5:10 NIV, read 1 Peter 5:6–10

Many would testify that being without work is as gut-wrenching an experience as they have ever had. We love the stability and security that a job gives us. We know where we belong at 8:30 on Monday morning. When that time comes around every week and we have no place to go, we can be thrown into a quagmire of anxiety.

No matter what I may be going through now, I can expect the best from God. The answers to my prayers may not come when I want them to. I may lose some financial assets. I may go through a gauntlet of personal emotional disruption.

But I don't have to worry about losing my relationship with God, either now or in the future. First, he says to bring all my anxieties to him. He understands every frustration, every emotion, every worry, every idea that even comes through my head. That is why I can bring it all to him.

Second, he reminds me that my future is assured. His final restoration will be far beyond just getting my old job back or getting set up in a new one. It will be made permanent by the greatest power in the universe.

One of the most beautiful images in the Bible is that

of Romans 8 where creation is described as waiting eagerly for Christ's final revelation as parents wait on tiptoe to see their child coming down the street in a parade. Likewise, I can eagerly expect that God's final resolution will eclipse every doubt, hurt, and fear. He has promised it in his Word.

*Thank you, Jesus, that I'm not alone. You're with me even as I think these thoughts. There's not a single problem I have that you haven't dealt with before. Thank you that I can boldly pray for the continued comfort and assurance I need for today. And tomorrow you'll be there for me too.*

# Learn to Help Others

*Praise God, the Father of our Lord Jesus Christ! The*
*Father is a merciful God, who always gives us comfort.*
*He comforts us when we are in trouble, so that we can*
*share that same comfort with others in trouble.*

*2 Corinthians 1:3–4 CEV*

I never intended to write a book like this. The initial
pages were hardly more than a way for me to get my feelings out on paper, where I could deal with them on a
conscious level. Reflecting on the Scriptures, applying
them to my experience and my feelings was a way of letting God help and comfort me.

Then the economy got worse and I found others who
were going through similar experiences in my industry,
in my church, and in my community. I'm not sure I
could have helped anyone in the first few months of my
crisis. The emotions were still too raw. I was still reacting
vigorously to my experience. I was still looking too
much for sympathy and comfort myself. I was still too
close to the experience to think objectively.

Slowly, though, the Holy Spirit and the Word cut
through the confusion. The comfort that God provided
made me more comfortable. I could then move more
into reflection instead of just reaction. If you find these
writings helpful, it is because I've received God's comfort. He moved me from needing so much help to being
able to help others.

Look for that to happen in your experience too. Be

aware of people who are worse off. Make yourself available to talk to others who are struggling. Work to comfort others whose pain you understand now. No one can make it alone.

*Dear God of all comfort, let me be a minister of the abundant comfort you provide. Let the calming spirit of your presence flow through me to others you put in my path. Make my experience a fruitful one as I reach out to comfort those I can influence.*

# Recommended Reading

*A Path Through Suffering,* Elisabeth Elliot, Servant Publications

> Elliot tackles the difficult subject of suffering head-on. There's good help here, especially when you feel you are at an all-time low.

*Decision Making and the Will of God,* Garry Friesen, Multnomah Press

> While Friesen presents all the major views on the subject, he also strikes off in a somewhat different direction than many authors. He suggests that, where the Bible gives no specific command, the believer is free to make wise decisions on the basis of broad scriptural principles.

*Disappointment with God,* Philip Yancey, Zondervan Publishing House

> One of the clearest and best writers around, Yancey compassionately and honestly tackles this subject that many writers shy away from. He thoughtfully asks and tries to answer three basic questions: Is God unfair? Is God silent? and Is God hidden?

*Facing Turbulent Times,* Gordon MacDonald, Tyndale Publishing House

> The author examines the lives of Joseph and Isaiah in a most-needed effort to demonstrate the principles

that one must follow to cope with turbulent times. At present this book is out of print and may not be available at most bookstores. Church libraries or Gordon MacDonald fans may be your best source for locating it. Perhaps some publisher will get it in back in print soon.

*Finding a Job You Can Love,* Ralph Mattson and Arthur Miller, Thomas Nelson Publishers
This could be called a kind of self-discovery book. It's a good tool to help you examine spiritual and emotional motivational factors in your work.

*Forgive and Forget,* Lewis Smedes, Harper & Row and Pocket Books
If forgiving someone for creating your job crisis is one of the issues you struggle with, Smedes's book is probably the best resource available. In a very readable style, he lays out the reasons forgiveness is necessary, no matter how badly you may have been wronged.

*How Long, O Lord?,* D. A. Carson, Baker Book House
Carson does a great job of making the book of Job applicable to the grief we face in a job crisis. His writing is challenging, instructive, and compassionate.

*If You Want to Walk on Water, You've Got to Get Out of the Boat,* John Ortberg, Zondervan Publishing
When you're ready to absorb a challenge to use your

gifts to the fullest, read this book. Ortberg creatively invites readers to go beyond their comfort zones and take the risks that will lead to the great adventures of the faith.

*Knowing God's Will,* M. Blaine Smith, InterVarsity Press
Smith systematically leads the reader through the Scriptures with questions and a study guide. He deals at length with the idea of guidance.

*Loving Your Work Ever After,* Phyllis Taufen and Marianne T. Wilkinson, Doubleday
If you like fill-in-the-blank worksheets, this book is for you. It has 72. It also has a lot of practical suggestions, such as how to write a standout resume and do an effective interview. It is set up in a readable, bite-sized format.

*Rebuilding Your Broken World,* Gordon MacDonald, Thomas Nelson Publishers
MacDonald has come through spiritual brokenness with a genuine, intense faith, and the reader feels it while reading the book. His is a testimony to the power of God's grace through a crisis that included a job loss as only part of a whole set of problems.

*The Call: Finding and Fulfilling the Central Purpose of Your Life,* Os Guinness, Word Books
If you are struggling with finding God's will for a career in your life, Guinness' book will help you rethink

the issues. His understanding and explanation of the significance of the idea of a "call" will be helpful in re-setting directions and goals for life.

*The Three Boxes of Life*, Richard N. Bolles, Ten Speed Press

While this title isn't nearly as well-known as *What Color Is Your Parachute?*, I find it an instructive perspective on the relationship of school, work, and play as they interrelate in all of life. Bolles's challenge is to avoid getting caught in only one of those boxes at a time.

*The Will of God as a Way of Life*, Gerald Sittser, Zondervan Publishing

Sittser shares his experiences of learning to understand God's will for his life while going through significant tragedy.

*Trusting God*, Jerry Bridges, NavPress

For Bridges the key to getting through a crisis is to know God and trust him. While using many practical examples, he attempts to expand the reader's concept of God. When we know him, we find it easier to trust him.

*What Color Is Your Parachute?*, Richard N. Bolles, Ten Speed Press

Harvard Business Review says of *Parachute*, it is "one of the finest contributions to the literature on life/work planning. . . . It serves to hold the reader's interest while showing that job hunting, self-assessment, and career planning need not be a dull, arduous, awesome task." Bolles, an Episcopal priest, gives a lot of alternative techniques to job hunting that substantially contradict traditional want-ad and resume methodology.

*Where Do I Go from Here with My Life?*, R. N. Bolles and John Crystal, Ten Speed Press
   A full-fledged workbook that can be used in conjunction or instead of *What Color Is Your Parachute?*.

*Where Is God When It Hurts?*, Philip Yancey, Zondervan Publishing House
   A slightly more basic approach than *Disappointment with God*. It has been a standard on the subject for years.

*Your Work Matters to God*, Doug Sherman and William Hendricks, NavPress
   Along with *Keeping Your Head Up*, this is one of the best books written of late to help Christians integrate their faith and work. It's very practical. A study guide is also available.

Richard Malone lives in Murfreesboro, Tennessee. He and his wife, Sue, have two sons, Dan and David. He is a graduate of Evangel College and Trinity Evangelical Divinity School. He currently works for Riverside Distributors as Vice President of Product Purchasing. His hobbies include swimming and bicycling.

Udacity          TAMU.edu
Saylor.org
Cousera
EdX